Pra

the **information** store
☎ 01603 773114
email: tis@ccn.ac.uk

21 DAY LOAN ITEM

- 2 FEB 2015

Please return <u>on or before</u> the last date stamped above

A fine will be charged for overdue items

CITY
COLLEGE
NORWICH

Practitioner Research and Professional Development in Education

Anne Campbell, Olwen McNamara
and Peter Gilroy

P·C·P
Paul Chapman
Publishing

Paul Chapman Publishing
A SAGE Publications Company
1 Olivers Yard
London EC1Y 1SP

SAGE Publications Inc
2455 Teller Road
Thousand Oaks, California 91320

Sage Publications India Pvt Ltd
B-42, Panchsheel Enclave
Post Box 4109
New Delhi – 100 017

Library of Congress Control Number: 2003109190

A catalogue record for this book is available from the
British Library

ISBN 0 7619 7467 9
ISBN 0 7619 7468 7 (pbk)

Typeset by TW Typesetting, Plymouth, Devon
Printed in Great Britain by TJ International Ltd, Padstow, Cornwall

Contents

Preface   *viii*

Foreword   *ix*
Stephen Newman

1 Research Traditions in Education   **1**
Introduction   1
Two crude traditions   2
Two more subtle traditions   2
Reflecting reflection   9
Notes   11

2 Researching Professional Development   **12**
The political context for teacher research and development   13
Your professional development   18
Interrogating the value of professional development activities you have
    experienced   20
Controlling your professional development   22
Teacher researchers   24
Further reading   26

3 Professional Identity: Who am I? What Kind of Practitioner am I?   **28**
The moving image   28
Exploring your professional development   30
Telling your story   35
Summary   46
Further reading   47

4 Identifying an Area for Research   **49**
Introduction   49
The first moves   49
Individual ways of approaching research   60
Concluding remarks   62

5   Finding, Reviewing and Managing Literature   65
    Types of literature   65
    Managing literature   67
    Searching for literature   71
    Reviewing your literature   78
    Further reading   79

6   Which Research Techniques to Use?   80
    Research: what research?   80
    Reflective writing, diaries, logs and journals   87
    Biography, stories and fictional critical writing   91
    Observation   93
    Interviewing   98
    Analysing the data from interviews   102
    Using questionnaires   102
    Conclusions   104
    Further reading   105

7   Critical Friendship, Critical Community and Collaboration   106
    The lonely researcher?   106
    How does critical friendship work?   109
    Critical community   118
    Mentors as support for research   122
    Further reading   124

8   Qualitative Data Analysis   125
    Introduction   125
    The broader picture   126
    Techniques for analysing qualitative data   129
    Further reading   145

9   Quantitative Data Management, Analysis and Presentation of
    Questionnaire Surveys   146
    Introduction   146
    Data management and coding   148
    Data analysis   159
    Data presentation   164
    Further reading   168

10 Writing up, Reporting and Publishing your Research   **169**
Writing up: genres, purposes and audiences   169
Legal and ethical considerations   172
Writing for a report   174
The research process   175
Writing for publication   177
Using literature   178
The process of writing   181
Pen-portraits: an alternative genre of writing   182
Concluding remarks   185
Further reading   186

11 Evaluating and Disseminating Research   **187**
The professional agenda   187
The mechanics of evaluation   191
Concluding remarks   198

Resources for Research   *199*
Harvard referencing: questions and answers   199
Summary report from the Friars Primary School: 'Improving Literacy:
    Intervention for Low-achieving Pupils'   205
Further reading   211
References   *212*
Index   *219*

Preface

There has been a major shift in the nature, content and location of professional development in the last five years. This has included a move away from courses and workshops to workplace and professional learning communities. This move has been accompanied by a gradual realisation of the importance of research-based professional development and research and evidence informed practice to promote teaching and learning and school improvement.

This book aims to support and prepare practitioners to undertake small-scale inquiries and research investigations. The processes of research and inquiry-based learning help teachers come to terms with the complexities and challenges of teaching as their responsibilities widen to include the notion of the teacher as researcher. This major shift in responsibilities has focused on teachers using and doing research, with a particular emphasis on examining how teachers' research can impact on teaching and learning. This emphasis is clearly related to the drive to raise pupil achievement and to related areas such as monitoring progress, performance management, inspection and collegiate and collaborative work for school improvement.

The idea for this book grew from the authors' teaching experience and day-to-day professional work with teachers and others in the caring professions. The book aims to open up forms of research for practitioners so as to develop critical appraisal and analysis skills appropriate to professional contexts. It will suggest activities and give support for doing and evaluating teaching by using authentic examples of teachers' research into professional issues. It aims to stimulate and promote teachers' narrative writing and autobiographical approaches to researching their professional lives. It also tackles quantitative data management and analysis procedures that are relevant for teachers and other professionals. It is envisaged that it could support those involved in performance management appraisals and threshold application.

Thus the book is firmly located in work with teachers and others concerned with understanding education within continuing professional development contexts. We consider that practitioner research lies at the heart of professional development and so it seems timely to produce a book that focuses on understanding the connections between this form of research and professional development.

Anne Campbell, Olwen McNamara and Peter Gilroy

Foreword

Stephen Newman

Teacher professional development has a higher political profile today than for many years, and links with appraisal and performance management may mean that at times professional development is seen as something to be endured rather than enjoyed. Yet as the authors of this book make clear, teacher professional development can take many forms, and a key aspect of successful professional development is the commitment of the participants to the activity. Such commitment is more likely if the focus of the development activity is chosen by the participant rather than imposed from the centre.

Choosing which development activity to pursue imposes pressures of its own. You may feel that you have nothing to say or that the research you want to do is of little significance. Perhaps you are overwhelmed by the different possible lines your research could take. You may feel daunted by the difficulties of juggling all your responsibilities, professional and personal. You may even feel that you are being a little bit selfish, wanting to pursue an area of interest which inevitably is going to involve sacrifices by yourself and others. These at least were some of the thoughts I had when, as a full-time teacher in a comprehensive school, I decided to pursue some research part time. Even now, some years after my official periods of part-time study were successfully completed, reading through this book I am relieved to find that these fears and worries are perfectly normal.

Taking the initial steps of pursuing research once those initial fears have been overcome (or even perhaps when they have not) brings to the forefront a plethora of further questions. Is there anyone who will be willing to supervise the work? What will I have to write? Will my ideas be hopelessly inadequate? How will I be able to cope with all the literature? What research methods would be appropriate? These and many other questions are addressed in this book. It is useful to be reminded of the many opportunities that exist for small-scale research for educational development which can provide not only valuable professional development in themselves but which may also provide a route into larger-scale research. The questions and checklists are helpful in looking at the range of opportunities that already exist, in highlighting areas which can be developed, and in developing techniques for making explicit aspects of professional identity. These techniques can help us as teachers to resist the view of professional development as something which is done to us by so-called 'experts', and promote the view that we can be active in choosing how we want to develop.

Having made the initial decision to pursue your ideas further it then becomes necessary to consider where you can best carry out your research and on what sort of course or activity. Of paramount importance it seems to me is the matter of finding someone to supervise your work with whom you are able to work well and who is able to act as one of the 'critical friends'. Here time spent at the beginning of your research will be time well spent. You will need to be able to trust your supervisor and accept the criticisms which you hope he or she is going to level at your work in order to help you to develop it. A poor relationship will sap your morale and your enthusiasm, and the quality of your work is likely to be the poorer as a result; on the other hand, a positive relationship should help periodically to reinvigorate your research, help you to focus your ideas (as you know they are going to be subject to close scrutiny) and promote your confidence in arguing your ideas.

In preparing to conduct your research it is worth giving some thought to the reasons which are going to provide you with your motivation. Motivation will be important; you may find yourself (as described in this book) writing late at night or early in the morning (and possibly both), and having to forgo some of the activities which, if it were not for your research, you would be able to enjoy. Motivation is, of course, very individual and may well consist of a number of inter-related factors which will help to give you the determination you will need and help to sustain you when you hit difficulties. Just like the results of educational research, your reasons for wanting to do research, and the factors that are going to help to motivate you, are likely to be complex; clarifying them in your mind will help you to persuade yourself and others that what you are doing has purpose and direction.

Let us assume that you have made a decision to conduct some research and have been able to meet someone who has agreed to supervise your work. Now is the time to start in earnest on the formal part of your work (assuming that you have been thinking informally about the issues hitherto). One point that I came to realise was very important to help me to progress was that it was pointless to wait for inspiration. So I can readily agree with the sentiment expressed in this book that it is important to write. Writing, I find, helps to develop my ideas and to clarify my thinking; drafting and redrafting help me to develop my ideas further. What you write may never make it into the final copy of your work but in working and in thinking through the ideas it is possible to find a line of argument which eventually turns out to be fruitful.

And what sort of writing you do can vary according to the time available and your alertness; note taking and following up references can be done when you are tired, so use quality time when you are alert for taking your arguments further and developing your arguments. But the general rule I had was that I would keep writing (writing notes, writing drafts, revising work) even when I felt I would make little progress; I came to feel that the 'slow times' were an integral part of the work, demanding of me the 99% perspiration which I hoped would eventually give way to the 1% inspiration.

Much of your writing will develop from reading. Access to the Internet and all the electronic resources available today makes the task of accessing resources a lot easier than it once was, but with the drawback that now the sheer quantity of material may be overwhelming. Getting to know the main libraries you will use, and how they work, will be time well spent. Similarly I quickly came to appreciate how important it is to keep an accurate record of every book or article consulted. Two minutes making an accurate note at the time of initially consulting a work can save hours later trying to find a 'lost' paper or book. I found it useful to make notes on my computer and to make and keep dated backups so that I could always go back through my archive to find the original source of any quotation or idea. I also found it important to make a note of which library I had found the book or article in and the shelf-mark of each book; this made going back to the original that much easier.

It is likely that in doing your research you will come across references which you need to follow up but which are only obtainable from elsewhere. Perhaps you will find some references impossible to trace, perhaps because they are incorrectly noted in your sources. This at least was my experience. Although initially frustrating, I came to enjoy pursuing lines of inquiry and tracking down a book or article which had almost been 'lost'. I was delighted by the care with which library staff (in the UK and abroad) and academic staff would try to help track down papers from 20 or 30 years ago, where perhaps only one copy remained in some dusty file. This camaraderie is part of what binds those working in what is sometimes called the 'academic community'. Becoming part of that community you will be attending meetings and conferences where you may meet people whose work you have read but whose faces are unfamiliar. This was my experience, made all the more enjoyable by the realisation that I could contribute and have my ideas scrutinised by others. Sometimes I was happy to participate as a silent witness to exchanges between well-known academics and to follow the cut-and-thrust of a lively academic debate. Either way, whether as contributor or witness, this involvement with those at the forefront of research is exciting and rewarding. This is an aspect of the academic community to which reference is made in this book which rings true for me. And the contrasts which research affords can be illuminating; an early morning meeting with my supervisor followed by a drive to my school for the rest of the day's work would see me switching thought mode from the later philosophy of Wittgenstein to the normal routines of school within an hour. But even here the insights given by my research enabled me to view the daily life of school in a new light.

Perhaps you wonder what your colleagues will make of your involvement in research. Perhaps some will see it as slightly bizarre. If so, this is something to relish, just as those who enjoy other interests relish them, interests which you may find bizarre. Variety is the spice of life. Some may be interested and eager to participate or to know more. Some may have done research previously and be eager to discuss your ideas and progress with you. But much of your research will be quite a lonely task, at least in terms of the physical presence of someone doing the work with you. But come to see the books and papers you will be using as the voices of colleagues in another room and it does not seem so lonely after all. And, of course, you will come to meet with fellow researchers, even if infrequently, who can help to offer the framework of critical support which can help to move your own work forward.

Making your research results public in some form is an important aspect of research and of professional development. The discipline of publication helps sharpen arguments and reduce confusion and errors and opens up your work to peer review, a vital role of the academic community. Not only is it professionally rewarding to see your work made public but it can also give personal satisfaction to you and those who have supported you through the sometimes lonely experience of research. It is also to be expected that, having completed your research, you will have conclusions to share with others; having your work published provides a way of formally presenting your ideas for this purpose.

Your involvement in research may result in some form of accreditation. It may also give you a lasting interest in your chosen area of study, to which you may be able to return at a future date or continue in another form after the official part of your research is completed. Other consequences of carrying out your own research for professional development are likely to include an increased scepticism (in my view, healthy) of many of the edicts handed down from 'on high' to the teaching profession, and a recognition (again, in my view, healthy) that the learning community is one which extends across formal institutional boundaries and that practising teachers have an important contribution to make. For reasons such as these I am delighted to have been asked to contribute this Foreword.

Perhaps reading this book will give you new ideas for research as part of your professional development. If so, the underlying message of the authors, it seems to me, is that you should have the confidence to take your ideas forward.

In memory of Helen Francis
(PG)

With thanks to all the teacher researchers
I have had the fortune to encounter.
My special thanks to Ian Kane for his 'red pen' work.
(AC)

1 Research Traditions in Education

OVERVIEW

This chapter introduces some of the key concepts used in the book by introducing you to some of the more important broad traditions of education research. This leads you into an introduction to the practitioner research movement, which underpins the ideas that form the core of this book.

Introduction

Let us assume that you have identified some aspect of your professional practice in your classroom that is puzzling you. You may have noticed that one particular technique you use to encourage effective learning does not appear to be working as well as it used to, or that another is working very effectively. You may have seen something in the news or read something in the educational press that reminded you of your own classroom or at least caused you to wonder how it might apply to your own professional situation. At this point you have taken the first step as a researcher in that you have identified an educational issue that might need resolving. We could generalise by saying that much educational research focuses on interesting puzzles that have been identified by practitioners.

The second step in the process is to carry out a small-scale study of the aspect of your professional practice in the classroom that is puzzling you. However, as a beginning researcher in education you may not realise that there are a number of research traditions in education and that you may find yourself operating within them without realising that you are doing so. It is important that you recognise the tradition you are perhaps unknowingly accepting, as each has various methodological advantages and disadvantages which feed through to your findings and conclusions. In fact, the practitioner research approach we have described above is itself just one tradition amongst many. These traditions are themselves worthy of research, as they hide puzzles that have a knock-on effect to the research they generate in ways that we will discuss in this chapter.

Two crude traditions

One of the most common ways of identifying traditions of educational research is to identify a distinction between quantitative and qualitative approaches to research. As the term suggests, quantitative educational research deals with measurement of quantities of some sort or another. If you studied for your teacher's qualification in the UK before the 1980s it is likely that at some point you will have been introduced to the so-called disciplines of education, in particular the psychology and sociology of education. There are still parts of the world where such an approach to preparing students for teaching flourish. Research within the psychology of education set out to make the understanding and improvement of education scientific, in that it would provide objective knowledge about education so as to allow for that knowledge to be used to improve the learning of pupils and the teaching techniques of teachers. Similarly, early forms of the sociology of education made extensive use of statistical analyses with, for example, pupil achievement being measured in quantitative terms.

There have been a number of criticisms of this approach to educational research, not least being the fact that education involves interpersonal relationships whose subtleties cannot easily be captured in quantitative terms. The argument being presented by such critics is that education involves issues to do with the quality and nature of these relationships, so educational research is uniquely qualitative. As such, objective scientific measurement of the activity is more often than not inappropriate as a quantitative approach to qualitative debates can rarely capture such inquiries, though they may be used to inform aspects of them.

Two more subtle traditions

In outlining the quantitative approach to education research we have referred to research being scientific and therefore producing objective knowledge. That conception of science is itself a particular tradition with a particular understanding of the nature of knowledge and one we now need to examine in more detail.

THE POSITIVIST, COMMONSENSE TRADITION

This is an approach to knowledge which is usually first referenced to August Comte's 1844 publication, *Discourse on the Positivist Spirit*. He argued that there were three broad ways in which natural phenomena can be explained, the theological, the metaphysical and, finally, the positivist, this last being an approach whereby natural events are properly to be explained by reference to empirically observable concrete phenomena. From that conception of how knowledge is to be gained comes what might be called the commonsense view of science.

This views scientific research as progressing through a series of steps as follows. The researcher begins with observations and experiments which produce facts which in turn allow a hypothesis to be developed. The hypothesis is further tested so that it can be confirmed and, once it *has* been confirmed, this allows the researcher to produce (or induce via a process termed induction, where one moves from some to all) a law which represents objective Knowledge,[1] Truth or Reality. This aspect of the research tradition is represented in the five steps presented in Figure 1.1. The final stage in this research tradition is to use the objective Knowledge that has been produced through the empirical process represented in Figure 1.1 to produce explanations and predictions based on that Knowledge by a process termed 'deduction' (see Figure 1.2).

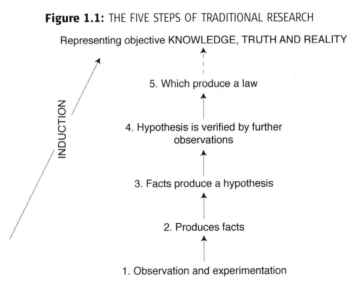

Figure 1.1: THE FIVE STEPS OF TRADITIONAL RESEARCH

Representing objective KNOWLEDGE, TRUTH AND REALITY

INDUCTION

5. Which produce a law

4. Hypothesis is verified by further observations

3. Facts produce a hypothesis

2. Produces facts

1. Observation and experimentation

Figure 1.2: THE SIXTH STEP OF TRADITIONAL RESEARCH

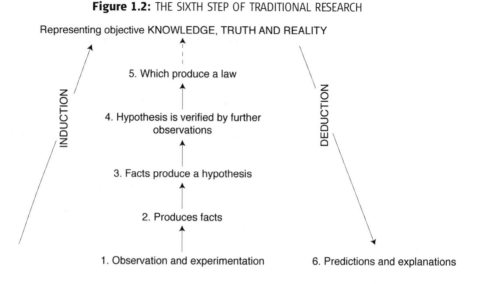

Representing objective KNOWLEDGE, TRUTH AND REALITY

INDUCTION

DEDUCTION

5. Which produce a law

4. Hypothesis is verified by further observations

3. Facts produce a hypothesis

2. Produces facts

1. Observation and experimentation

6. Predictions and explanations

Illustration: the positivist tradition of research

If you decide to carry out an inquiry which has the following features:

◆ you identify a hypothesis;

◆ you use observations to prove your hypothesis;

◆ you make use of the facts identified by your proof to identify some sort of objective Knowledge; and

◆ you deduce a universally applicable conclusion

then you are clearly operating within a positivist tradition of research, irrespective of whether your work is to be seen as quantitative or qualitative research (or even a mixture of these two approaches).

An example drawn from the English context shows how this tradition might be relied upon to justify practice. Let us assume that after a number of observations of young children successfully learning to read in, say, Singapore, it has been suggested that it is necessary to have highly structured reading hours provided on a daily basis, with equally rigidly structured activities to follow. This hypothesis to explain why it is that Singaporean children read so effectively is then tested by observing as many young Singaporean children's reading lessons as possible, to produce the law that all young children can be taught to read effectively in this way. Given this empirically derived Knowledge it is then but a small matter to deduce the prediction that the reading abilities of young English children will be improved by using these methods. In this way an apparently sound, evidence-based policy decision can then be introduced to the teaching profession.

This tradition has at least three major problems which you need to be aware of, as they will seriously compromise your findings if you do not find ways of addressing them.

Problem 1

The first step in this tradition depends upon observation. But observation itself depends upon what we are interested in observing. That is, we do not approach situations, especially social situations such as those we find in the classroom, free of certain assumptions about their nature. These assumptions allow us to select from the wealth of information that we are presented with only those details that interest us, so we are not observing in some pure, assumption-free manner. Consequently, the kinds of knowledge that we create as we observe social situations are inevitably influenced by the assumptions we bring to bear on the situations we observe and try to make sense of.

Problem 2

Figure 1.1 shows clearly that induction, the move from some to all, underpins the move from singular observations to universally applicable objective Knowledge. Yet the number of observations that are required to justify the move from some to all, from the finite to the infinite, would have to be an infinite number too. As finite creatures ourselves this is clearly impossible. The critical effect of this basic problem on positivism has been described thus: 'That the whole of science . . . should rest on foundations whose validity it is impossible to demonstrate has been found to be uniquely embarrassing' (Magee, 1973: 21).

Problem 3

Figure 1.2 indicates that deduction, the move from all to some, underpins the move from universally applicable objective Knowledge to the singular application of that Knowledge. The difficulty here is that the crucial distinction between something being *true* and an argument being *valid* is being blurred. Here are two examples of logically valid arguments, valid in that they move from 'all to one' in a logically valid way:

A

1. All books on research methods are boring.

2. This is a book on research methods.

3. Therefore this book is boring.

B

1. All writers on research are female.

2. The author of this chapter is a writer on research.

3. Therefore the author of this chapter (Peter Gilroy) is female.

Step 1 of both arguments are assumptions but only argument B's assumption is demonstrably false. However, that does not prevent argument B's conclusion being valid but untrue. The point here is that even if there were to be universally applicable Knowledge about the social world you have to take very great care in relating it to particular situations, as deduction alone will not guarantee the truth of your conclusions.

We said that you would need to address these three problems if you wanted to work within this positivist tradition. If you do not then you might produce conclusions to your research that assumed that the observations you made were untainted by the assumptions you bring to bear to select one set of observations from another. This would have the problem of preventing you seeing that your conclusions were inextricably linked to the assumptions that underpinned the observations you selected as significant. The second problem we have identified makes it clear that you cannot justifiably make a universal generalisation from specific observations, which would clearly influence the way you treated your findings. The third problem suggests that the move from all to some, the reverse of the problem of induction, is one that might be valid but you would still need to test for its truth, irrespective of its validity.

These three problems seem to lead towards a modification of positivism which is so drastic that it in effect represents a rejection of the tradition. The key modification is to reject the attempt to produce universal conclusions and to accept the need to operate at a more specific level of inquiry. We identify this tradition as contextualism, and will now examine its key features.

THE CONTEXTUALIST TRADITION

There are a number of different approaches to educational research that could be accommodated within this broad tradition, but before identifying them we first need to establish the key features of the tradition itself. The central identifying feature of the tradition is its emphasis on context as providing the background to any social inquiry, none more so than educational inquiry.

A key thinker in this area is Karl Popper, who claimed to have solved the problem of induction 'in 1927, or thereabouts' (1971: 1). He accepted that it is not possible to justify universal Knowledge by reference to finite observations but, rather, that instead we have to falsify them by testing them to destruction. In addition he accepted that observations are dependent upon the various assumptions made by the person carrying out the observation or, as he put it: 'Observation is always selective . . . these observations . . . presupposed the adoption of a frame of reference . . . a frame of theories' (1974: 46–7). He argued that inquiry is caused by recognising that a trial solution that had been offered up for falsification (or error elimination) would eventually produce a further problem that would require error elimination and so on, with the process of inquiry being never ending. Consequently the knowledge that is created is provisional, always the possible object of further attempts to falsify it. This approach is represented in Figure 1.3.

Figure 1.3: THE PROCESS OF INQUIRY

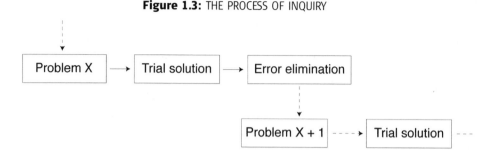

It is Popper's notion of a frame of reference that we term *context* and which provides the basis for the observations that allow for research to begin. It is in this sense that we talk of observations being context dependent. It follows that any conclusions we draw from such observations are also context dependent, as are the application of those conclusions.[2] So this research tradition emphasises the context-specific nature of all stages of its methodology, from the initial formulation of a particular problem through to whatever tentative and highly provisional conclusions might be produced which are also, of course, context specific.

If we apply this to the example previously identified regarding the use of research on the method used to teach young Singaporean children's reading, we can see immediately the importance of context. For example, if the children's social background was such that they had considerable assistance and support in reading at home, if the Singaporean culture is one that encourages reading in various ways other than those actually observed then these, amongst many other context-specific factors, have been ignored: and that is to leave aside the various complex contexts in England where a straightforward application of the methodology of one context's success to another context or set of contexts might be quite inappropriate.

The drawback to this tradition of research is the difficulty of providing any meaningful generalisations as conclusions to the research. However, from the point of view of a contextualist that is not so much a drawback as a major advantage, for generalisations are part and parcel of the positivist tradition. Another criticism might well be that the conclusions are so specific to a context that they have little or no standard against which to judge their truth, unless you are also part of that context. Again, the contextualist would not see this as a problem but rather as an inevitable aspect of social inquiry, with descriptions of social phenomena accepted as *ringing* true, rather than *being* true.

Teacher-initiated research, which as we shall see is part of teachers' continued professional development, is likely to follow the contextualist tradition. To begin with it is unlikely than many teachers will have the resources to carry out the large-scale surveys or case studies necessary to produce the sheer quantity of data required to allow for some form of research within the positivist tradition. More to the point, Popper's 'problems' and 'error eliminations' are more likely to create further problems within the context of a class or set of classes that a teacher is responsible for. So for both practical and methodological reasons it is likely that teachers will be drawn towards a contextualist tradition once they begin to carry out research.

We now need to examine in a little more detail the practitioner research movement.

Reflecting reflection

Perhaps the first person to argue that teachers, by dint of the fact that they were teachers, were also researchers, was Lawrence Stenhouse. In opposition to those who wished to impose curriculum developments on teachers, with teachers seen as little more than technicians delivering a curriculum 'product' that others had designed, he argued that curriculum development was a process whereby teachers translated their educational values into practice. It follows that curriculum development (which, of course, includes teaching a particular curriculum) is a form of research, with teachers researching their own practice so as to come to a better understanding of the values they are relying on to inform and improve that practice.

Although not referring to Stenhouse directly or, for that matter, to teachers in any detail, an American thinker, Donald Schön, has been seen as developing these ideas further. The key concept he introduced into educational debate was that of the reflective practitioner, with 'practitioner' being used to include a very wide range of professions, including architects, psychotherapists and lawyers. His arguments for the way in which these professions develop their practitioners have been used by many in teacher education to explain what they regard as the key feature of being a teacher, namely reflection on practice. Indeed, it would be an unusual course which nowadays did not at some point make mention of reflection or reflective practice. But what is meant by reflective practice and how does it connect to the teacher as researcher?

Schön introduces his seminal work, *The Reflective Practitioner: How Professionals Think in Action*, by stating that the book is an 'exploration of professional knowledge' (1983: vii). He continues by setting up a straightforward distinction between two accounts of what he calls professional knowledge. The first he terms Technical Rationality and he argues that, for various reasons, such an approach to accounting for professional knowledge should be rejected, not least because it cannot account for the 'artistic, intuitive processes which some practitioners do bring to situations of uncertainty, instability, uniqueness and value conflict' (1983: 49).

The second is a form of knowledge which he terms Reflection-in-Action. Schön argues that in everyday life we have a tacit knowledge of aspects of our behaviour and this is revealed by the rule-governed way in which we act. This 'knowing as revealed by actions' is often quite spontaneous and the actors concerned are usually unaware of it (1983: 54). Part of what it is to be a good practitioner is to be able to bring this tacit knowledge to the surface by a process called reflection-in-action, by thinking through one's actions as one is producing them in the thick of one's professional situation. This behaviour, reflecting critically on one's actions whilst at the same time acting, is what he identifies as reflective practice.

There has been much discussion around Schön's work (see, for example, Gilroy, 1993; Newman, 1999) but in the context of this chapter it should readily be seen that it can easily be assimilated to what we have termed the contextualist tradition. The reflective practitioner is by definition a researcher, researching not just their own professional context but, crucially, researching that context as they act within it. Moreover, they may be doing this at a tacit level without realising that they are adjusting their behaviour to accommodate the complex situations they are acting within. It is in this sense that such individuals are researchers, researching their everyday practice *as* they practise.

In Schön's terms, our book is intended to provide the understanding and tools which will help to improve your reflective practice, by allowing you to see how you might (consciously) critically reflect on your (subconscious) reflections. In so doing you will, with Stenhouse, be behaving as a teacher researcher.

Notes

1. The use of the capital is intended to indicate the objective status of such Knowledge, as opposed to knowledge which is more subjective.
2. For more details of this position, see Edwards *et al.* (2002: ch. 3).

2 Researching Professional Development

OVERVIEW

This chapter explores the current context affecting issues surrounding the professional development of teachers and develops an argument for a particular approach to teachers doing research. It promotes the concept of teachers as practitioner researchers and their efforts to research thinking, practice and professional development. It seeks to highlight the relationship between doing research and developing professionally and to argue that researching classrooms and school contexts is a vital part of teachers' professional development. It argues for the evolution of a new perspective on continuing professional development policy and provision.

It seems timely to explore understandings of the forms that teachers' professional development may take, to understand better how the processes of development work. This chapter investigates notions of professional development and proposes that investigation and research of professional development are a worthwhile activity for teachers to undertake in pursuit of improving and developing practice in teaching and in education in general. As a preparation for moving into the issues raised in this chapter, you should attempt to address the following questions:

◆ Why has professional development become a major focus of government policy?

◆ What constitutes professional development?

◆ What roles do autonomy and self-determination play?

◆ What roles do research and investigation play in professional development?

◆ How can teachers start exploring their own professional development?

◆ What impact could research have on me as a professional?

We are also increasingly coming to understand that developing teachers and improving their teaching involves more than giving them new tricks. We are beginning to recognise that, for teachers, what goes on inside the classroom is closely related to what goes on outside it. The quality, range and flexibility of teachers' work are closely tied up with their professional growth – and the way they develop as people and as professionals (Hargreaves, 1992: ix).

The political context for teacher research and development

Teaching today takes place in a world of rapid change and development and teachers are expected to meet high standards of teaching and raise levels of achievement in schools and colleges. During the last 15 years or so, education has been the subject of intense accountability measures, especially in England which has seen the implementation of a National Curriculum and the introduction of a national programme of testing arguably more detailed and demanding than any other national programme.

As measures to inspect schools and appraise teachers have been introduced under the banner of 'modernising' teaching, teachers have often felt a lack of ownership and a lack of self-worth (Ruddock, 1991). Within the context of 'rolling reform' and piecemeal implementation, the professional development of teachers has become a high-profile, politically 'hot' issue. Civil servants, politicians, professional associations, private sector companies, universities, schools and local politicians, all are stakeholders in teachers' professional development. All teachers are required to engage in professional development; to identify, document, record and evaluate it as they cross through the barriers of qualified teacher and induction standards, grapple with targets for performance management, submit threshold applications or bid for research scholarships, international exchanges, professional bursaries and sabbaticals.

This phenomenon is not restricted to the UK. Cochran-Smith and Fries (2001: 3) describe the scene in the USA, where: 'there have never before been such blistering media commentaries and such highly politicised battles about teacher education as those that have dominated the public discourse and fuelled legislative reforms at the state and federal levels during the last five years or so.'

The battles referred to are those of opposing sides, one trying to professionalise teaching and link this to raising standards in schools, the other trying to deregulate teacher preparation and development and setting out to highlight the lack of connection between teacher qualifications and pupil achievement. Cochran-Smith and Fries (2001: 13) made an important point that: 'the way the problem of teacher education is conceptualised in the first place has a great deal to do with the conclusions that are drawn about the empirical evidence suggesting what policies are the best solutions for reforming teacher education.' There would appear to be a great deal of commonality in the state of teacher education and development in both the UK and the USA.

The professional development of teachers has been a target of government policy. It is contained within an official publication, *Learning and Teaching: A Strategy for Professional Development* (DfES, 2001). There has been a gradual recognition over the last ten years or so of the importance of continuing professional development (CPD), as the English government has launched initiative after initiative in schools and teachers have tried to meet the challenges of rapid change. Literacy and numeracy strategies followed the juggernaut of the National Curriculum and testing, then for example, education action zones, Excellence in Cities, Beacon schools, flagship schools, training schools, specialist schools and colleges, city academies and networked learning communities, to name but a few.

Similar initiatives have happened and are happening in the USA and Australia. Many European countries are engaged in whole-scale review of teacher education and teacher support and development structures in order to enter the European Economic Community or to bring their provision up to date. There is a move to locate the majority of professional development and professional learning in schools in order to embed initiatives and give schools and teachers the responsibility for organising and managing development.

These are difficult times for teachers. Far more public accountability is demanded than ever before and that accountability is increasingly more visible in league tables, inspections, media coverage of schools and international comparisons.

In England, it would appear from ministerial speeches and from policy documents such as the CPD strategy (DfES, 2001) and more recent policies aimed at moving professional development funding to schools that individual schools and classrooms are to become 'learning communities' and the main, key, future sites of professional development. In Scotland, a recent major initiative supporting teacher development has established the 'chartered teacher', a well qualified 'advanced' teacher who will engage in research and professional development and promote these amongst colleagues. The 'raising standards' agenda dominates the professional preparation and development of teachers in England, and initiatives that support teachers must demonstrate how they will address the raising of pupil achievement. It is an assumption that better prepared teachers mean better achieving pupils, and current initiatives are predicated on improving teaching and learning in classrooms by supporting teachers in their professional development. There would appear to be a tension between personal professional development needs and the needs of the school or department. This tension has been largely ignored, though an identification of individual needs features prominently in the proposed implementation in many of the new initiatives or innovations at central government level. Some would argue that teachers' professional development has been revived as an issue due to recruitment and, in particular, retention issues in the profession (Eraut, 1999).

A variety of support has been promised: classroom assistants, new technological support, scholarships, bursaries and the provision of good-quality CPD. Normally, however, these are not available to all teachers and schools as an entitlement. Teachers and schools have to make bids and write proposals, sometimes to gain financial support or to match funding to participate in development activities. The culture of 'bidding' and proposing projects has arrived in the UK as a recent import from the USA, increasing the divide between the 'haves' and the 'have nots'. Whilst a climate of diversity offers flexibility it can also result in inequalities of provision and entitlement for pupils, teachers and schools.

Highly politicised debates have also been imported, as referred to by Cochran-Smith and Fries (2001) in their article which examines how 'the evidentiary warrant-empirical versus ideological', the 'political warrant – good versus private good' and the 'accountability warrant – outcomes versus inputs' are intended by advocates of competing agendas to add up to and capture the 'linguistic high ground of common sense' about how to improve the quality of America's teachers. They conclude with a cautionary note that unless there is debate about the underlying ideals, ideologies and values in relation to the evidence about teacher quality and about the discourse of teacher education reform, there will be little progress in understanding the politics of teacher education reform and the competing agendas.

With regard to the English context, Whitty (1999) refers to the tensions between regulation or state control of teachers' work and the apparent shift back to 'licensed autonomy' through the establishment of a General Teaching Council (GTC). We have, in both the English and American contexts, a situation where there is seemingly a great deal of central control of the profession but also a move to deregulation in terms of entry to the profession and access to professional development. Whitty argues that a 'third way', or a way that is different from the state control model and the 'traditional professionalism or self-governance' model, needs to be found in order to move forward. He calls this alternative 'democratic professionalism', where teachers would set up alliances with parents, pupils and members of the community, seemingly not a long way away from some of the current proposals for learning communities and networks, but he asks: 'In the light of recent history, my question would be – is either the state or the profession willing to face up to the challenge?' (1999: 10).

In his Foreword to *Learning and Teaching: A Strategy for Professional Development*, David Blunkett, the then Secretary of State for Education and Employment, states that: 'I believe that professional development is above all about developing extraordinary talent and inspiration, and especially the classroom practice of teachers, by making sure that they have the finest and most up-to-date tools to do their job' (DfES, 2001: 1). Teachers' professional development toolkits will have to have more than the physical tools which teachers use. Does a toolkit need to include personal qualities such as enthusiasm, creativity, joy and passion? If not, the toolkit would arguably be less than adequate. Hargreaves (1992: ix) believes:

> Teachers teach in the way that they do not just because of the skills they have or have not learned. The ways they teach are also grounded in their backgrounds, their biographies, in the kinds of teachers they have become. Their careers – their hopes and dreams, their opportunities and aspirations, or the frustration of these things – are also important for teachers' commitment, enthusiasm and morale. So too are relationships with their colleagues – either as supportive communities who work together in pursuit of common goals and continuous improvement, or as individuals working in isolation, with the insecurities that sometimes brings.

Defining professional development is not an easy task, highly dependent on the cultural and socioeconomic climate prevalent at any one time. Certainly at the time of writing, in the early twenty-first century, teachers' professionalism has been somewhat demeaned by the intense media coverage of what goes on in classrooms and schools and by the number of government interventions in what teachers should do and know. Day (1999) agrees with Hargreaves when he writes about 'teachers' development being located in their personal and professional lives and in the policy and school settings in which they work' and sees teacher development as lifelong and a necessary part of teaching. Day (1999: 2) has ten precepts about professional development which underpin his work and which span the following points. These may serve to illustrate a set of principles for good-quality professional development arising from research.

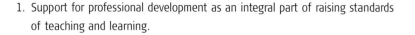

Illustration: the principles for good-quality professional development

1. Support for professional development as an integral part of raising standards of teaching and learning.

2. Teachers as models of lifelong learning for their students.

3. Lifelong learning in order to keep up with change and innovation.

4. Learning from experience is not enough.

5. The value of the interplay between life history, current development, school contexts and the wider social and political scene.

6. The synthesis of 'the heart and the head' in complex educational settings.

7. Content and pedagogical knowledge cannot be divorced from teachers' personal, professional and moral purposes.

8. Active learning styles which encourage ownership and participation.

9. Successful schools are dependent on successful teachers.

10. Planned career-long development is the responsibility of teachers, schools and government.

Implicit in the above precepts is the notion that professional development takes many forms, from the solitary, unaided, daily reflections on experience, to working with a more experienced or knowledgeable practitioner, observing and being observed, professional discourses, and attendance at workshops, courses and conferences. There has been little research that has focused on the nature and quality of CPD, apart from Day's seminal work and review of research (1999). Recently the government commissioned a team of researchers from Manchester Metropolitan University and Education Data Surveys to undertake a national baseline survey of approximately 2,500 teachers' perceptions of CPD in order to gain information about the range and quality of CPD in England which would help them plan initiatives for the future (Hustler *et al.*, 2003).

Your professional development

It may be useful at this point to list the main types of professional development activity in which you have participated in the last three years. Try to provide a variety of different types. Annotate your list with perceptions of how valuable and effective you found the different activities and types of events. This may help you later in Chapter 3 when it is suggested that you might compile a *curriculum vitae* in order to review your professional identity.

An American study of approximately 1,000 teachers' opinions of effective professional development across the USA was recently published from which a number of interesting findings can be gleaned (Garet *et al.*, 2001). The research focused on mathematics and science teachers' self-reported accounts of the effects of different characteristics of professional development on their learning. Results indicate core features of professional development activities that have powerful effects on learning and changes in classroom practice:

◆ Focus on content knowledge.

◆ Provide opportunities for active learning.

◆ Have coherence with other learning activities.

It was found that, through these core features, the following structural features significantly affect teacher learning:

- The form of teacher activity.

- Collective participation of teachers from the same school, grade or subject.

- The duration of the activity.

Example: types of professional development

In order to help you compile your list, some headings are suggested below of types of professional development:

- Classroom-based development activities, such as team teaching, observation, coaching, group discussion.

- School-based development activities, such as joint planning and design of units, leading or participating in a session for school staff, writing a school policy.

- More formal school-based input by a visiting 'expert' (literacy or numeracy specialist or other such person).

- Attendance at a short course (e.g. half day, one day/two day, 10 sessions) organised by the LEA, a regional or national body, university or consultant.

- Longer-term course with accreditation (e.g. Open University, local university or professional/subject association).

In summary, it was concluded 'that it was more important to focus on the duration, collective participation and the core features (i.e. content, active learning and coherence) than type' of learning (Garet *et al.*, 2001: 936).

Whether an activity was traditional (e.g. workshops, events external to classroom and school) or more modern (e.g. using strategies to support change in classrooms such as mentoring, coaching, joint planning – i.e. events on-site) was less important than sustained, content-focused, coherent, active learning. One major challenge identified for provision of high-quality professional development is cost. The results demonstrate: 'in order to provide useful and effective professional development that has a meaningful effect on teacher learning and fosters improvements in classroom practice, funds should be focussed on providing high quality professional development experiences' (Garet *et al.*, 2001: 941).

There are a number of lessons to be learnt from this article, not least the need for collective participation in professional development. Current CPD initiatives in England seem to favour individual teachers as the focus for initiatives (requiring them to apply for funding or search out the appropriate activity for themselves) but also requires all teachers to participate in prescribed national training for literacy and numeracy. The advent of appraisal and performance management for all teachers may have forced teachers to focus on their professional development activities, but direct linking of pupil progress to pay may prove to be a wrong move in trying to reprofessionalise the teaching force. The Hay McBer Report (2000), whilst espousing a managerial approach to teacher development, indicated that a degree of autonomy was important in teacher development, and this is supported by Whitty (1999) in his identification of the current struggles over professionalism.

Interrogating the value of professional development activities you have experienced

In the light of the above findings consider whether you agree with the following statements. Use the data produced as a basis for discussing the review of your professional development at a later stage. Consult the list you compiled earlier and try to find out what made the professional development activity worth while.

After participating in this activity, consider what you think the main features of professional development should be. Do your colleagues agree with you? Find out by asking them whether they agree with the above statements and write up your thoughts. These will provide useful data to help contextualise your later thoughts on researching professional development.

Exercise: professional development

Which of the following statements applies to you?

- ◆ I find that my learning is more effective when the activities I undertake are linked and coherent with previous experiences.

- ◆ I prefer to listen rather than do.

- ◆ I have enough knowledge for my teaching; what I need are more tips and strategies.

- ◆ I like variety in my learning, otherwise I will get bored.

- ◆ I favour approaches which focus on the content of teaching and aim to improve and increase my subject knowledge.

- ◆ I prefer to be actively involved in my learning, experiencing new activities and learning new ways of doing things.

- ◆ It would be useful to have colleagues on the same sessions so that we can talk about it afterwards and develop our ideas further.

- ◆ I like quick, relevant inputs and then to move on to something else.

- ◆ It does not matter whether the teachers in sessions have anything in common as we all have our different ways of doing things anyway.

- ◆ I like going to several sessions with the same people in order to get some continuity of discussion and to get sustained development.

- ◆ I prefer sessions to have varied formats to suit different types of activities.

- ◆ It does not matter if all the sessions are the same format as long as it is effective.

Controlling your professional development

Changes in the last 20 years would appear to have resulted in a decrease in teachers' professional autonomy and seem very distant from Stenhouse's (1975: 144) ideas of 'autonomous professional development through systematic self study ... and through questioning and testing of ideas by classroom research procedures'. However, it could be argued that some of the current initiatives, such as teachers as researchers and school-based networks for learning, may fulfil aspects of the vision Stenhouse had of professional communities of teacher researchers. Day (1999) also espouses the establishment of networks as powerful sites of teacher learning but pragmatically also identifies the need to invest in teachers and schools in order to provide sustained professional development for teachers. Autonomy in the context of professional development does not mean 'going it alone' but refers to the rights of practitioners to design and shape the types of learning and continuous professional development activities they identify, either through collective or individual evaluation and analysis of their practice.

Who now decides what teachers need to know and how their professional development should take place or of what it should consist? As can be surmised from earlier evidence above, much of teachers' professional development activities in the recent past in England at least have, since the introduction of the National Curriculum, been driven by the needs of government initiatives, policy and a somewhat punitive inspection regime. The heavy emphasis on raising standards within national strategies and projects with prescribed content and pedagogy, whilst important, would appear to allow little autonomy and ownership of such policies and practices for practitioners.

But not all is gloom. The tide seems to be turning, with school self-evaluation, peer review and 'lighter touch' inspections being the order of the day. Day (1999), for example, advocates a synchronisation of institutional and personal professional development approaches in order to maximise the opportunities for change and development in schools. It has often been suggested that appraisal systems would be the best way for this to happen, but research has shown this to be problematic. Wragg *et al.* (1996) found that there were ongoing tensions between school and individual needs, limitations in funding for appraisal and problematic issues of confidentiality and personal change. It will be interesting to research and investigate whether current appraisal and performance management initiatives support and facilitate change and a high quality of professional development activity.

Many researchers of teachers' professional development feel that self-determination and autonomy are key aspects or hallmarks of professionalism (see Woods, 1994; Day, 1999; Elliott, 1999). An example of such an approach would be MacBeath (1999) in his work on school improvement and effectiveness, where he argues for a balance between external and internal collaborators and evaluators, and for ownership and self-determination as key components of successful developments and successful schools.

Exercise: autonomy and self-determination

Consider the questions below in order to explore your own ideas about autonomy and self-determination and to build up a better picture of your ideas about professional development, which can be used later on in Chapter 3:

◆ How could you identify your professional development needs? Is it solely the responsibility of the individual or are there school, regional and national perspectives to consider?

◆ What kinds of needs do you have?

◆ How can you be helped to identify your professional development needs?

◆ What role should internal colleagues and external 'experts' or consultants play?

◆ Should whole departments/faculties/schools/other groups of local teacher specialists or year-group teachers contribute to and organise activities for professional development purposes? Should this happen or not? You may like to develop an argument.

◆ What kinds of products should there be from professional development activity? Is it always necessary to have a product?

◆ What role do you envisage for networks and partnerships? How could links with existing networks and partnerships (e.g. initial teacher education and training (ITET) and cluster groups of schools) work and to what end?

◆ What professional development do you experience from the various roles you may undertake as a teacher? For example, many teachers mentor trainees, and newly qualified teachers (NQTs) develop, through rigorous questioning, a healthy review and evaluation of their practice. This might include a reminder that subject knowledge is an important aspect of teaching and needs constant refinement and renewal. Roles such as moderator or leading teacher for a core subject offer other opportunities for professional development.

◆ What would you like to research as a teacher? Have you considered what you would like to find out about in your classroom or school?

Teacher researchers

The value of teachers undertaking research has yet to be fully appreciated. There are many examples of how teachers can become researchers evident from the early days, in Lewin's (1948) work and Stenhouse's (1975) vision of teacher researchers in professional communities, but there is still a debate about teacher research and 'real' research in the academic arena. Currently there is also a debate about 'evidence-based practice' and pressure on practitioners to use evidence to inform their practice in similar ways that have been developed in medical contexts. Elliott (2001) develops a view that current versions of this position (Hargreaves, 1997, in particular) subscribe to an unquestioning commitment to an outcomes-based view of education and lack sufficient attention to educational theory and its contribution to conceptualising aims and objectives. Elliott's view would seem to support Stenhouse's (1975) position that 'teachers using research are doing research'.

The current focus on teacher research is not new. For decades, teachers supported by, and encouraged by, universities and colleges of higher education, and sometimes funded by LEAs, have engaged in action research, practitioner research, collaborative inquiry and teacher research in schools and classrooms in order to improve teaching and learning and to develop and refine the curriculum and teaching practice, and to innovate and evaluate their teaching (see, for example, Stenhouse, 1975; 1980; Elliott, 1974; 1981; Nixon, 1981; Hopkins, 1985; Hustler *et al.*, 1986). In England during the 1970s and 1980s teachers were often funded, through secondment to universities, to undertake research-based courses at universities and colleges, and a considerable amount of unpublished teacher research was produced.

The emphases on evidence-based practice, the opportunity to apply for funding for classroom and school-based research and the focus on raising standards through teacher research are new. One concern about recent and current initiatives, expressed by Elliott (1999: 1), is that strategies to promote teacher research and evidence-based practice may not support the empowerment of teachers, but may be an attempt to 'establish an epistemic sovereignty to legitimise its [the government's] interventionist policies to drive up standards'.

A further concern is the imprecise nature of teacher research. Teachers may subscribe to the view, along with some critics of practitioner research, that the only legitimate research is large-scale quantitative research that arrives at clear-cut, measurable outcomes and conclusions. This type of research may be viewed as positive if it also matches or endorses government policies. For many novice teacher researchers, there is a strong pull to believe that research is a straightforward process and that any struggle with conflicting evidence proves to be difficult. But research into the complex processes of teaching and learning is not always neat and tidy; it is frequently messy and inconclusive. There is often a naïve belief that teacher research may solve all the problems of complex classrooms.

The notion of criticality, of teachers being able to take a critical stance about what they choose to research and what they find out from their research, is arguably of crucial importance to how current teacher research initiatives are viewed within the research community and within the teaching profession itself. Key factors in the development of a strategy to promote critical thinking and teacher research would include: autonomy and control of research questions and design of projects by the teacher researchers; a high quality of support for research projects; robust processes of self-monitoring, critical reflection and evaluation; and transparent procedures for dissemination and debate of research projects and findings.

However, whilst accepting the paradoxical nature of teacher research, in that it could be in danger of becoming anything and everything, Sachs (1999: 41) argues that: 'teacher research has the potential to act as a significant source of teacher and academic professional renewal and development because learning stands at the core of this renewal through the production and circulation of new knowledge about practice.' Sachs also argues that there are three distinct forms of teacher-initiated school-based inquiry, 'teacher inquiry, action research and collaborative research', all of which have relevance to those wishing to improve their practice. In teacher inquiry, she identifies new roles such as critical friend, new structures such as writing teams who may work on tasks such as documenting practice and new opportunities for disseminating and creating a culture of inquiry into professional development (see Chapter 11). This notion of creating a new culture is attractive to all who wish to understand more about teaching and learning and who wish to harness research to improve policy and practice. Sachs also raises similar issues to Elliott (1999) concerning the tensions in action research arising from the relationship between theory and practice for teachers who value their 'craft knowledge' above the theories underpinning teaching practices. We must not lose sight of the importance of teachers' views and 'the power of the personal' with regard to teachers as researchers (Campbell, 2002) nor of how, as Hargreaves (1992) reminds us, 'teachers' work is deeply embedded in their lives and developing the teacher therefore involves developing the person, developing the life'.

The seeds of teachers researching their professional development are planted in various initiatives such as practitioner, professionally focused and action research programmes and degrees in universities and colleges and in research networks and the newly formed local networks springing up in the regions. But these networks and initiatives need nurturing and strengthening to grow into vibrant and strong learning communities and partnerships where critical friendship and critical communities can flourish. The role of higher education personnel in teacher research is a vital and key one, providing support for research through partnerships with teachers, schools, LEAs, consultants and funding bodies.

In conclusion, it may be timely to remind ourselves that if we are to retain and sustain teachers in the profession in the future, then providing them with a voice and empowering them through active participation in research which allows them to investigate and shape the knowledge base of their teaching may be a key factor in defining their professionalism and underwriting their commitment to education.

Further reading

Dadds, M. (2001) 'Continuing professional development: nurturing the expert within', in J. Soler *et al.* (eds) *Teacher Development: Exploring our own Practice.* London: Paul Chapman.
Marion Dadds' chapter was written just before the publication of the 2001 CPD strategy in England and provides a commentary on models of continuing

professional development. The collection in Soler *et al.* (above) is a very useful resource for those wishing to investigate teachers' professional development further.

McNamara, O. (2002) 'Evidence-based practice through practice-based evidence', in O. McNamara (ed.) *Becoming an Evidence-based Practitioner*. London: RoutledgeFalmer.
Olwen McNamara's chapter opens up the issues explored through a TTA-funded project where teachers, LEA advisers and university tutors worked together in a school-based research consortium. She tackles the sea change in practice and attitudes to research in the last 20 years and draws on data gathered from teachers as to what counts as research and what an evidence-based practitioner might look like. Other chapters are written by teachers themselves or in collaboration with university tutors and focus on actual research projects undertaken.

Pirrie, A. (2001) 'Evidence-based practice in education – the best medicine', *British Journal of Education Studies*, 49(2): 124–36.
This article suggests that the desire to find evidence to support classroom practices may result in a belief in 'toolkits' for teachers as a legitimate outcome of research. The dangers of overlooking the complexity of doing research could mean oversimplistic conclusions being generated from such an approach.

3 Professional Identity: Who am I? What Kind of Practitioner am I?

OVERVIEW

This chapter will suggest ways that teachers, either in groups on courses, in networks or clusters of schools, or as lone practitioners wishing to improve practice or prepare for a new job, or as a part of performance management procedures or as part of an assignment for an MA, or for whatever reason, can begin to think, write, explore and talk about their professional identity. The underlying assumption is that undertaking research in this area will improve teachers' teaching and learning strategies. The chapter provides sets of questions, suggested activities and devices to facilitate exploration and research.

Identity should not be seen as a stable entity – something that people *have* but as something that they *use*, to justify, explain and make sense of themselves in relation to other people, and to the contexts in which they operate. In other words identity is a form of argument. As such it is both practical and theoretical. It is also inescapably moral: identity claims are inevitably bound up with justifications and belief (Maclure, 2001: 168).

The moving image

The image of teaching and teachers has been the subject of much media interest and reporting for several decades. Until quite recently when either a Damascan conversion or a supply crisis has brought about a change of heart and of tone, teachers have been attacked and vilified on many fronts as the politicisation of education has caused an intense scrutiny of what happens in schools and classrooms and brought about the imposition of a 'raising standards' agenda on the teaching profession. But there is little sense of 'argument', in the public domain, as Maclure indicates above.

It could be argued, echoing Maclure, that teachers in England have undergone a series of professional identity crises as bandwagons such as the National Curriculum, performance management and their involvement in initial teacher training have lumbered through schools' and teachers' lives. Teachers have become 'deliverers' of the curriculum. Their performance is appraised and managed and targets are set for the future; they train novice teachers through a plethora of routes into teaching as 'mentor', 'trainer', 'provider', 'professional tutor' or 'teacher-tutor'. The commercialisation of education and the advent of a new managerialism (Hargreaves, 1994) have been cited as resulting in a loss of autonomy and a confusion of identity for teachers. Bolam (1999: 1) identified the main features of a 'new public management' as including: 'less teacher autonomy, increased line management of teachers, delegation of tasks to para-professionals, more distinct managerial and bureaucratic layers, reduced collegial involvement, centralised decision making and emphases on target setting and "national" accountability.' It is entirely understandable that teachers feel confused. It is arguably time for teachers' roles and responsibilities to be reviewed, in an exploration of values, attitudes, knowledge, skills and pedagogy that could be reflected in a professional identity which acknowledges the complexity and scope of the job of teaching in the current context. The teacher's image now is one which involves a loss of autonomy, a lack of self-determination and a culture of audit and excessive accountability.

This chapter will suggest ways in which teachers can actually explore their professional identity through an investigation of, and research into, their professional history in order to illuminate and identify future areas of development. There will be exercises to undertake in writing, thinking and talking. In particular, the power of narrative, biography and telling stories about professional development will be discussed. Maclure (2001: 167) asserts that:

> There is a lot of interest these days in the personal dimensions of teachers' lives – in knowing what teachers are like and what makes them tick . . . As a result, informal, person-oriented genres such as narrative and biography, autobiography, life history and anecdote have become quite widely accepted within educational research and professional development.

She cites the work of Connolly and Clandinin (1990) on stories of experience and narrative inquiry as an emerging paradigm in research into teacher identity. This approach to researching teachers' lives through stories is further explained in Chapter 6, which discusses the types of research approaches and techniques open to those wishing to research their professional development and to improve their practice. She quotes Ball and Goodson (1985: 13) 'opening up the sealed boxes within which teachers work and survive' in support of the promise of greater explanatory power offering better links between teachers' individual lives in classrooms and schools and current social structures. From her research into teachers' lives and jobs, she suggests that identity can be an organising principle in teachers' jobs and lives and that teachers' identity claims can be seen as a form of argument, 'as devices for justifying, explaining and making sense of one's conduct, career, values and circumstances'.

It is exactly how these devices, and others enabling practitioners to research their practices, thinking, attitudes and beliefs, might look and work that this chapter wishes to examine and illustrate. In summary, it is the intention to enable practitioners, through writing activities and group discussion, to:

- identify the beliefs and attitudes which underpin their practice;

- engage in a systematic process of individual and collaborative reflection and analysis and in an individual review of professional learning and development;

- participate in self-appraisal, evaluation and action planning;

- investigate relevant literature in the field of professional development; and

- write accounts of narratives and stories about professional development both past and future.

Exploring your professional development

Figure 3.1 sets out a process by which teachers can explore their professional development. The starting point is straightforward. Experience of working with teachers researching their professional development indicates that some exploration

Figure 3.1: EXPLORING PROFESSIONAL DEVELOPMENT

Researching professional development processes

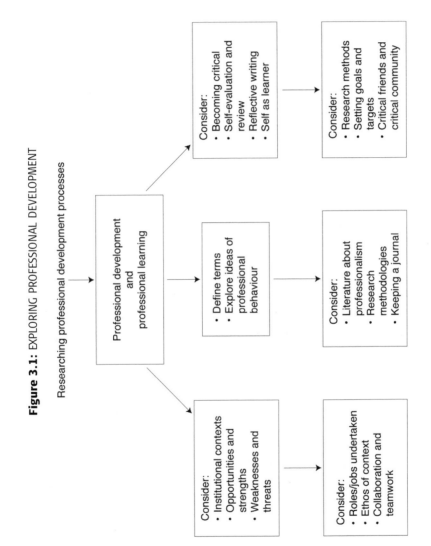

Professional development and professional learning

Consider:
- Becoming critical
- Self-evaluation and review
- Reflective writing
- Self as learner

Consider:
- Research methods
- Setting goals and targets
- Critical friends and critical community

- Define terms
- Explore ideas of professional behaviour

Consider:
- Literature about professionalism
- Research methodologies
- Keeping a journal

Consider:
- Institutional contexts
- Opportunities and strengths
- Weaknesses and threats

Consider:
- Roles/jobs undertaken
- Ethos of context
- Collaboration and teamwork

of the literature and teachers' ideas of 'professionalism', 'professional' and 'professionality' will make a good place to begin the process of talking, thinking and writing about professionalism. Hoyle (1974) suggested that: 'professionalism refers to the strategies and rhetoric employed by members of an occupation in seeking to improve status, salary and conditions, and professionality refers to the knowledge, skills and procedures employed by teachers in the process of teaching.' Tomlinson (in Thompson, 1997: 11) says that teachers feel they need to convince the public that they are a 'proper' profession and often try to demonstrate their professionalism through being seen to 'agonise over ways to better understand the needs of their pupils and about ways to better teach their pupils'. Whitty (1999: 10) concludes his paper on teacher professionalism in the twenty-first century with the following wake-up call which could make a good starting point for discussion:

> Throughout the last twenty years or so, teachers and teacher educators have been understandably preoccupied with issues of short term survival in the face of an unrelenting flow of new initiatives and inspections. It is now time to begin working with others to develop new approaches that relate not only to the legitimate aspirations of the profession but also those of the wider society – and that must include those groups within civil society who have hitherto not been well-served by the professions or by the state. At a rhetorical level, that does not seem a million miles away from the thinking of the present-day unions or even New Labour. But in the light of recent history, my question would be – 'Is either the state or the profession willing to face up to the challenge?'

Undertaking the process of researching professional development as suggested in this chapter will involve considering the notions of professionalism and professionality. It may be useful to undertake a discussion and writing activity based around some questions to ask about the above concepts. How do these definitions relate to your own thoughts? It may be helpful to start writing about some of the questions above in order to explore professional identity. An entry in a diary or log that addresses the questions below might be a good starting point.

Writing about oneself as a practitioner is often difficult because it can feel like stating the obvious. It is useful at times to have a particular audience in mind. As part of the early stages of exploration of attitudes and beliefs and practices it is useful to write a brief pen-portrait of oneself in order to share it with another like-minded practitioner – for example, a colleague engaged in a similar research project, a member of the course you are attending, a person in the local network. The idea of sharing your pen-portrait is to encourage the colleague or partner to explore issues in an informal interview or documented conversation.

Exercise: exploring professional identity

The following are questions to address as a starting point for exploring professional identity:

◆ Are there currently struggles over professionalism and professionality (see definitions above)? If so, what are they?

◆ Are teachers being deprofessionalised or reprofessionalised? Consider Tomlinson's point about choosing the process by which you will teach. Is that autonomy being eroded in the present climate within which you work? Is it a core part of being a 'professional'?

◆ Is there a 'new professionalism'? Does it empower teachers? Or is it a 'new managerialism'?

◆ What view is held of explicit standards for teaching that are used to manage and assess performance?

◆ What challenges are there in the current climate for your professional autonomy?

◆ Do some teachers have more autonomy than others?

To help you write about yourself and address the question 'What kind of teacher am I?', we would suggest writing up a short *curriculum vitae* (CV) before embarking on the pen-portrait of yourself. The usual reason for compiling a CV is to apply for a job. What is suggested here is a somewhat different sort of CV, one in which you would not only chart your career to demonstrate the different roles and experience you have had but also one where you can explore ideas and reasons for moves and professional development. It should, none the less, help you when the time comes actually to apply for a job and a CV is required. The following guidelines are offered in support.

Learning aid: compiling a
developmental CV and a pen-portrait

Your personal details:

◆ Name, address, telephone/fax/email, age, gender.

Your professional details:

◆ Where and when were you educated as a teacher?

◆ Dates and location.

◆ What qualifications do you have?

◆ Awards and dates.

◆ What experience of teaching do you have?

◆ What areas of the curriculum have you taught?

◆ List subjects and areas taught with details of age groups.

◆ What posts of responsibility have you held?

◆ List promoted posts and responsibilities.

◆ What interests in education do you have?

Your professional development details:

◆ What professional development activities and processes have you been involved in?

- List and provide dates and duration of activities. Give details of whether you contributed to or led any of these.

- List any non-teaching activities or part-time teaching in other contexts which could support your development.

Other relevant information:

- List your current and past interests.

- Are there any other related interests or experiences that enhance your profile?

- What external responsibilities have you had?

- List any external roles you may have undertaken, such as examiner or moderator.

Having completed your CV, you can now move to a pen-portrait, which is different from a CV.

Telling your story

Teachers have personalities and these personal qualities, attributes and behaviours affect the way they teach and see themselves as teachers. Hargreaves (1992: ix) stresses the importance of teachers' backgrounds and life histories to the development of their teaching:

> Teachers teach in the way they do not just because of the skills they have or have not learned. The ways they teach are also grounded in their backgrounds, their biographies, in the kinds of teachers they have become. Their careers – their hopes and dreams, their opportunities and aspirations, or the frustration of these things – are also important for teachers' commitment, enthusiasm and morale.

'Core' questions, adapted from Smyth (1987) and presented below, are intended to aid the writing of a pen-portrait.

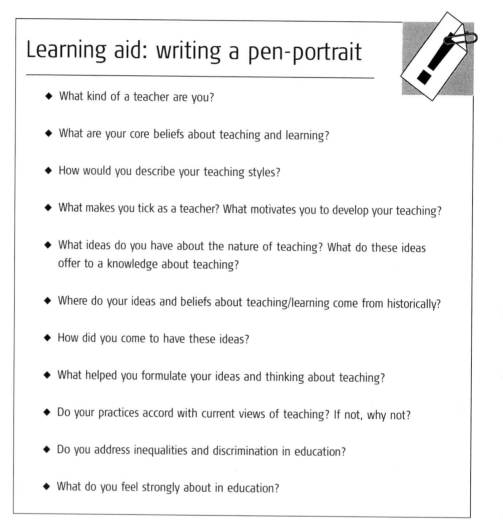

Learning aid: writing a pen-portrait

◆ What kind of a teacher are you?

◆ What are your core beliefs about teaching and learning?

◆ How would you describe your teaching styles?

◆ What makes you tick as a teacher? What motivates you to develop your teaching?

◆ What ideas do you have about the nature of teaching? What do these ideas offer to a knowledge about teaching?

◆ Where do your ideas and beliefs about teaching/learning come from historically?

◆ How did you come to have these ideas?

◆ What helped you formulate your ideas and thinking about teaching?

◆ Do your practices accord with current views of teaching? If not, why not?

◆ Do you address inequalities and discrimination in education?

◆ What do you feel strongly about in education?

The next stage in this process of researching your professional development is to exchange your writing with a colleague, critical friend (see Chapter 7) or partner, and then to formulate some questions for an informal interview with each other. The benefits of using another practitioner are various, another pair of ears and eyes, critical support and challenge and a different and more objective perspective on your ideas and views which opens up new doors and windows of opportunity. Some guidance for this informal interview is given below and further, more detailed, advice is given in Chapter 6. After reading your partner's writing, jot down your initial ideas about this person as a teacher. You are now in a position to design your informal interview schedule. It may be worth considering tape recording the session, not for transcription purposes but for authenticity of report and for checking against your understanding of what happened. Some questions to help you construct an informal interview are given below.

Learning aid: questions to aid informal interviews about teaching

- What do you think are his or her core beliefs about teaching and learning?

- What else would you like to know about his or her beliefs and attitudes?

- What questions will you ask to elicit more information and to help your partner articulate and develop more fully his or her answers?

- Does the information you have been given have any gaps or areas that are vague?

- How does your partner define 'professional'?

- Are there any points to pick up on for discussion?

Following the informal interview it would be useful to write up a summary of the main points arising. Alongside this brief account of the interview it would be helpful also to provide an analytical commentary that gives a synopsis of your interpretation of your partner's core beliefs and what you think might be some challenging issues to address in the future.

For the purpose of illustrating and modelling the process and supporting those who are new to this particular type of writing, extracts are presented below from:

- a pen-portrait

- an account of an interview

◆ some analytical comments on that interview.

PEN-PORTRAIT

Illustration: extracts from teacher P's pen-portrait

I have always subscribed to a model of teaching in which the pupils are encouraged to take some responsibility for their own learning. I have a firm belief in autonomy and ownership as an important part of the learning process. Through active participation in learning students/pupils can be empowered and can gain confidence as learners. I have tried to establish environments in my classrooms that allowed students/pupils to make decisions about their work – how they do it and when they do it.

This, however, is becoming more difficult as the curriculum and the way it is taught is becoming more prescribed. I also believe that first hand experience and using pupils' real life experiences is a good starting point for education.

During the 1980s when I did my teacher training there was little pressure from the government as to what or how to teach and I was allowed to develop my own ideas about teaching. I was heavily influenced in my own teaching by the models of teaching I experienced early in my career. I think having good, clear, detailed planning is essential for good teaching, but also being flexible is important. The teachers I saw in the 1980s had enthusiasm, energy and enjoyed teaching. They worked together a lot and went on courses together to improve their teaching. There was a lot of cross curricular work around then and I think the pupils enjoyed what they did a lot more when there was an element of choice.

When I think about it, I suppose that what I learned in college when I was a student teacher linked with what I believed anyway – it agreed with a set of principles about how to help children learn.

I feel strongly that children should be able to reach their potential and it is the teacher's job to raise their expectations of what they can do and that there should be adequate funding for all schools and classrooms regardless of where they are located. I find it hard to deal with inequalities in my classroom and in school and would like to learn how to deal with this in more effective ways. I like working with enthusiastic people who think learning is fun and who are not stuck in a rut. I have been lucky to work with colleagues who have helped me and worked alongside me to improve my teaching – this I find very motivating.

INTERVIEW

A set of questions was designed by teacher P's partner to help elicit more information in an informal interview. A selection of these questions and teacher P's answers is documented below.

Illustration: an informal interview

I: Can you explain more why you believe that autonomy and ownership are important in the learning process?

P: If children are too dependent on others and in particular the teacher, this causes them to lack confidence in their own initiative and their ability to instigate their own learning. It perpetuates one model of learning where the pupil is the recipient of knowledge that is transmitted from the more knowledgeable teacher. While imparting knowledge can be one of the roles of a teacher there are other roles that involve the facilitation of opportunity to explore and investigate alternative answers. It also creates a dependency on the decisions that a teacher may make instead of encouraging children to make decisions about how and what to learn.

I: Can you describe the sort of learning environment in your classroom that allows pupils to make decisions?

P: A learning environment which allows children to make decisions would feature choice of activity and the facility to organise one's own time. Organising a schedule of work to be covered for part of the day would allow for children to be flexible and would also allow them to develop planning and organisational skills which are so important for independent study in later years. Teaching children research skills so they can find things out for themselves as and when they need them would also be part of a flexible learning environment. Even with very young children choices can be made available as to which activity to do first and second on the day.

I: Can you explore the ways in which curriculum and teaching styles are becoming more prescribed?

P: Much of the Literacy Strategy in particular lays down what is to be 'covered' in each year group and also how it should be taught. Whilst it is useful to have help with planning, I do feel it is an intrusion to be told to download good lesson plans from the Internet. I like to be able to tailor my planning to meet the needs of the children in the class. There are many individual differences and children learn at different rates and paces. Setting targets for individuals and groups seems to have taken over my life. I don't have time to teach due to having to itemise all the targets. It all seems to have got out of control.

I: What sort of inequalities are there to deal with in classrooms?

P: Many children come to school at different starting points, due to differing pre-school experiences and differing abilities. Some children have had many advantages due to stable social and economic factors in their family backgrounds. Having the right kind of experiences, resources, staff with expertise in learning support, support for parents and carers to consolidate approaches developed in school would make a big difference. What seems to be happening is that schools which are good at bidding for extra money seem to be getting more and more while those who for one reason or another do not succeed in bidding get less and less. The gap between schools is widening and that affects the stability of staffing. It is obvious that some schools in inner city areas, with disadvantaged pupils are losing out – so where are the equal opportunities there? Anyway I think it should be about combating poverty, racism, exclusion and gender inequality rather than equal opportunities.

COMMENTARY

After the informal interview, a commentary can be given by partners that will then raise some further questions or provide feedback.

Illustration: commentary

Your answers reveal a strong commitment to active learning approaches and pupil independence and responsibility for learning. It might be useful in the investigation of your development to research how you maintain and sustain your commitment to these principles in the current climate of 'prescription' and central direction of curriculum and teaching styles. How have you developed and adapted your teaching to accommodate the 'new' emphasis on coverage of curriculum and the highly structured literacy hour?

What evidence do you have that your classroom learning environment does promote independence, choice and flexibility? How could you monitor that? Would it be possible to illustrate and demonstrate that independence and flexibility have a positive effect on pupil learning and pupil attitude as much of what you say infers that it does?

You obviously feel strongly about the inequalities in the school system. How could you provide more qualitative data about this? What case studies could be collated to illustrate and illuminate the problems and potential solutions?

The commentary opens up future research questions and areas and stimulates further responses in writing and in discussions. The partners are acting as 'critical friends' for each other, providing support and challenge for developing thinking and practice (see Chapter 7 for a fuller exploration of this role). One of the aims of this writing and interview exercise is to tackle how 'tacit knowledge' of practice can encourage practitioners to become unthinking and routine. Schön (1983) argued that reflection enables us to examine our practices and underlying assumptions in order to identify why we need to change our practices (see Chapter 1). Day (1999: 22) develops a powerful argument that reflection by itself is not sufficient for professional development to occur, stressing the need for collaboration and dialogue with other practitioners or facilitators as 'Reflection lies at the heart of inquiry, but whilst this is a necessary condition it is not sufficient in itself.'

Day develops Schön's model of reflection and devises ten challenges of inquiry that cover a comprehensive range of issues facing teachers as inquirers and learners. The relevant section is referred to in the further reading at the end of this chapter. Day

(1999: 47) concludes his challenges by making strong links between the professional and the personal and between inquiry-based learning and professional development supported by institutions:

> It should always be remembered, though, that reflection on teaching is not simply a cognitive process. Like teaching itself, it demands emotional commitment. It will involve the head and the heart. Perhaps the greatest challenge for individuals and organisations is to ensure that both of these are nurtured in systems designed to improve the quality of teaching and learning for teachers as well as for students.

SWOT ANALYSIS

Another way of reviewing where you are with regard to your professional development is to undertake a strengths, weaknesses, opportunities and threats (SWOT) analysis. SWOT is a useful tool to appraise the internal and external factors that influence a context or individual's performance. It can take the form of an audit, usually laid out as a box of competing areas:

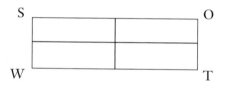

Strengths: What is going well? What is positive about the present situation? What are your current strengths?

Weaknesses: What is not going well? What is negative about the present situation? What are your current weak areas?

Opportunities: Consider the workplace situation and what it can offer to you as opportunities. Think also of the wider economic, political or social environment and what can be offered as opportunities. What is there in the resources or staffing situation that could offer you an opportunity?

Threats: What threats are there for you in the current workplace? Consider the wider economic or social climate and identify any threats which may affect you.

FORCE FIELD ANALYSIS

Another technique for studying a situation that you would like to investigate with a view to changing the practice or direction of your current professional future is that of force field analysis. Lewin (1947) first described this method of studying change which is based on the observation that, in general, a situation can be described as a balance between two types of forces, those of *driving* and *prompting* and those of *restraining* and *resisting*. The process has been adapted and developed over the years by many tutors and trainers and involves identifying the *driving* forces and the *restraining* forces you experience and then considering the strength of these forces and the influence that each force exerts on the situation.

Change can be brought about in three ways. By:

1. increasing the forces *prompting* change;

2. reducing the forces *resisting* change; and

3. a combination of (1) and (2).

Force field analysis can give insight into the nature of the role of teachers and the challenges facing them as they engage in professional development activities both in the workplace and at other venues.

There are a number of benefits in undertaking a force field analysis, not the least of which is that of reviewing the tactics and strategies in a systematic way. It is often best done with a critical friend or a trusted and experienced colleague or mentor who can give critical feedback in order to develop your thinking and approaches to difficult situations where there is conflict and differences of opinion.

DIARY AND STORY WRITING

Other ways of investigating and writing about professional identity can be undertaken through diary writing and story writing. Some extracts from teachers' writing are given below to illustrate a variety of approaches.

Kennedy (1996), writing about herself as a developing professional, gives a glimpse of her history and outlines how she is reviewing her practice as a teacher:

> For the first five or six years of my teaching career it was very exciting. I couldn't understand why some teachers weren't enthusiastic any more. Change wasn't a bad thing! Then, when change became the norm and lost its impetus, I began to find myself questioning the underlying philosophies of the many changes. I began to realise I was in conflict with much of what I was being asked to do. Yet I did not have the confidence and had only partial understanding of my own values to construct valid arguments against the imposed changes. I began to moan! I felt that if I was questioned, which rarely I was, about why I followed certain strategies in the classroom, I would be on very shaky ground. Yet I had managed to secure a management post and my responsibilities were increasing. I know I needed to do something for me.

Following 'doing something for herself', which was undertaking an action research course, she had the following comments to make:

> I have come to change my view of professional development and I am sure I will continue to recognise other aspects which at the moment I have not begun to articulate. The whole area of tacit knowledge has been quite a revelation. As I stated earlier, I have begun to look in a more disciplined way at my professional development after becoming disillusioned and dissatisfied with the view of development as acquiring new skills. I now know teaching is far more complicated than that. I knew as Polyani (in Holly, 1989) states: 'We know far more than we can put into words; we sense and understand more than we can describe.'

> I have found such research [researching professional development] difficult and until I read Smyth's (1991) book I found my journal entries rambling and unfocussed. Smyth offers four processes to develop and sustain a critical form of teaching:

Describing – (what do I do?)

Informing – (what does this description mean?)

Confronting – (how did I come to be like this?)

Reconstructing – (how might I do things differently?)

Kennedy then goes on to describe how she applied this structure to her teaching of drama and documents how using these four organising principles helped her to liberate her ability to uncover much of her knowledge about how she teaches. The experience of researching her own professional development has been a powerful experience and she claims has increased her self-esteem, having led her to become a more critical reader and a better facilitator of teachers' professional development.

This is a putative story of success, in essence, not dissimilar to that of Dadds' (1995) depiction of Vicky, action researcher. Dadds employs action research techniques in her case study of one teacher to illustrate the validation of teachers' action research and teachers' writing about her experiences and the contribution these make to teacher researchers' professional development. There are strong links across the professions, evidenced by Bolton's (2001) work on reflective writing in the health professions. There is much evidence that exploring and researching one's professional identity results in a type of professional development that goes beyond the acquisition of new tricks or techniques, however valuable they may be, to a more deep, 'therapeutical' type of professional development. Sikes *et al.* (2001) discuss how writing about 'critical incidents' in teaching can help teachers investigate and construct their professional identities and as a result affect changes and developments in teaching. Campbell and Kane (1998: 139) fashioned their data collected from and by teachers into a fictional critical writing methodology to increase teachers' access into stories that raised issues about the professional preparation and development of teachers, and concluded that:

> Exploring the edge of school-based teacher education, through fictional critical writing and tale telling has, we hope, stimulated interest in further research and investigation ... As well as opening up the personal, ethical, moral and human side of teacher and student experiences of partnership ... Readers may also identify and relate to characters, perhaps even recognise in them traits of a well known tutor, teacher, student, or pupil. Or self.

A short extract from Campbell and Kane's (1998) fictionalised accounts of school-based training is presented below to illustrate the methodology. The narrator is a tutor in university department of education:

> The phone call which I had just answered from Derek Wilson, the head of Jemima Johnston Primary School, asking me if I could make a Staff

Development Day four weeks hence, had triggered off my memories of Paula and her placement there almost three years earlier . . .

The first inkling I had that one of my more thoughtful, caring, student-centred decisions had gone badly wrong came with the phone call from Tom. Tom is not my favourite mentor. It is not that he doesn't dedicate himself to the task of mentoring; he does, almost obsessively so, and he keeps copious notes. He also writes copious notes on the student files whenever he gets hold of them. Sometimes he gets hold of them by rummaging in their bags and cases when they are not there. It used not to matter whether they were there or not until the year when one of our more assertive students bit his head off when he went into her Tesco bag. Indeed she barely stopped short off biting his hand off . . . Some students have found him a good mentor – usually those with few ideas of their own and a poor self-image . . . This time, however, the phone call heralded a complaint, not about Tom. About me. Now Tom, along with his other qualities is a direct descendant from Uriah Heap. His complaints about students, while carrying very clear messages about the shortcomings of our courses, our deficiencies of preparation, our poor quality students and our inadequate tutors, always come obsequiously packaged.

Through fictionalising data, writers can amalgamate traits and characteristics from a variety of people participating in the research and develop scenarios and vignettes that illuminate and illustrate complex situations and allow the portrayal of conflicting positions and ideas. It is hoped that readers will be tempted to try some of the suggestions in this chapter in pursuit of a better understanding of what their professional identity is, what makes them 'tick' as a teacher and, as Thomas (1995: 20) hopes: 'to move from writing to reflection to accepting the possibility of a personal professional response which has as its focus the classroom and then widens its lens out beyond the school to a consideration of the moral purposes of education – the imagined future.'

Summary

The routes above will hopefully lead to a more informed view of teaching, teachers and their professionalism and professional development. Beneath the exercise of researching one's professional development, lies a principled motivation. It was argued in the beginning of this chapter that teachers were suffering from excessive change and innovation overload. One damaging consequence of these phenomena has been that in-service education and development (or CPD) have become things that are 'done' to teachers. Reference was made to one teacher's account of the heady days when teachers used to go on courses by choice so as to improve their practice. The element of choice in professional development has been systematically diminished. If the pendulum is to swing back more towards autonomy or, at least, self-determination, then teachers must truly know what it is that they feel that they need. Whilst hunch and instinct will always be valuable tools, a more systematic approach to self-evaluation could play a very important role. Certainly performance management review is systematic and structured. Lest it lead to apparent unwelcome conclusions about what is required for one's further professional development, an equally systematic marshalling of self-determined needs should prove important so as to resist – or validate – top-down prescription.

Further reading

Day, C. (1999) 'Teachers as inquirers', in C. Day *Developing Teachers: The Challenges of Lifelong Learning*. London: Falmer.
This chapter gives a comprehensive overview of adult/teacher learning which is based upon an in-depth consideration of reflection. It discusses the 'emotional' commitment that teachers develop in their work and professional development and sets ten challenges of inquiry.

Bolton, G. (1999) 'Stories at work: fictional-critical writing as a means of professional development', *British Educational Research Journal*, 20(1): 55–68.
This article will be of interest to those wishing to find out more about fictionalising data and fictional-critical writing as a methodology. See also Gillie Bolton (2001) in the references for a more in-depth look at reflective writing.

Bottery, M. (1996) 'The challenge to professionals from the new public management: implications for the teaching profession', *Oxford Review of Education*, 22(2): 179–97.
Michael Bottery refers to a 'new public management' emphasis on such things as explicit standards/measures of performance, greater emphasis on output controls, the break-up of large entities into smaller units, market-type mechanisms, the

introduction of competition and a stress on professionalised 'commercial style' management.

These three very different readings build on the ideas of notions of professionalism, inquiry-based practice and narrative and fictionalising methodologies.

4 Identifying an Area for Research

OVERVIEW

This chapter is based on a discussion held by the authors of the book as they attempted to discover a topic they could research. The discussion is structured around the key themes that are a part of any attempt to identify a research topic.

Introduction

Three people came together for a recorded 60-minute discussion to identify a research topic. We present edited selections from the transcript that was produced to illustrate the way in which even experienced researchers have to cover similar issues to those which you will have to address. In passing it is worth noting that if you are thinking of tape recording interviews and then transcribing them, the complete transcription of this 60-minute discussion took just over five hours, an allocation of your time that you will have to think carefully about if you decide on transcribing a complete interview.

The first moves

To begin with you will need to *identify a research topic*. If you're lucky you will already have something very clearly in mind, but if not then you will need to play around with ideas and establish quite what it is you want to research. In what follows you will see Anne obviously had something she wanted to research and, through a process of discussion, that something becomes clearer.

Illustration: identifying a research topic

Anne (A): If I start the ball rolling. I've been thinking about the way in which professional development can take place within school and the way in which colleagues can be helped to put together their professional development portfolios. This could be almost like kite-marking their professional development in a relationship with a higher education institution. I suppose I'm thinking about something similar to Investors in People – the school seen as a professional development school that has undergone a process to provide quality professional development for its members of staff. So, I'd be looking at something that helped to research ways that a school might do that, with a school's professional development programme running alongside the more formal certification and might feed into it if a teacher wanted to.

Olwen (O): So you're talking of something that is driven by higher education (HE)?

A: No. The school is – well yes, HE would have a role in first of all identifying what was going on and then helping the schools to document it. And if you're talking about quality then you have to talk about learning outcomes, and you have to talk about structures and processes for managing these outcomes within the school. I suppose I'm talking of it as higher education having quite a big stake in it but the schools themselves operating the process with some kind of annual quality assurance mechanism.

Peter (P): But we seem to be moving well beyond a small and manageable cluster of schools. Instead of, presumably a couple of primary schools and a secondary school, and maybe a HE institution, the way you're talking, Anne, it is a much, much bigger project than that.

A: Yes, I was thinking that perhaps several groups of schools, whether just contained within the North-West, or whether you try to get some friendly groups in other parts of the country – because if you're going to make an impact on policy you need large numbers of research sites. Maybe we want to do something much smaller, but I would've thought that even if you could have a group one side of the North-West, and another group another side of the North-West and perhaps a third group somewhere else completely different, it would add to the project. I think the issues, say, in the rural schools for instance are going to be different than those in city schools. I was thinking maybe two, three, four clusters.

O: But that's a very much the 'done to' model, and really that's against the modern idiom isn't it? Its all about ownership and not being alienated from the decision making progress when it comes to managing your own, or your school's, CPD portfolio.

A: But there is an interest I know because I've talked to you about the network learning community I'm working with – ten schools – and they are very interested in this. They want help because they don't think they can do this themselves, but what they also want is the quality assurance, or the kite mark, from a local university. This is the scale of things beginning to get bigger. These schools are talking about not just teaching staff, but of course teaching assistants, and anybody that works in the school actually accrediting their professional development. They're saying really that there's more crying need for teaching assistants because they're already training them in schools themselves, and no there's no recognition of this. But of course you're talking there at National Vocational Qualification (NVQ) level rather than at degree level. That's something else that I was thinking about, looking at talking to open college federations of FE because I don't think unis are involved with NVQ's.

At this point you can see that not only are there problems with identifying a topic but also inevitably there are problems regarding the scale of the research topic, which has grown from examining CPD practices of teachers in a very limited number of schools to include all staff in schools in at least three widely differing locations. It is a common problem with a research topic that, fired by the interest and excitement of a good idea, you can find yourself going well beyond what you can manage without being part of a large research team.

What now happens is the initial idea leads on to another which attempts to reduce the *scale of the proposal*, which is then discussed further.

Illustration: the scale of the proposal

P: That idea though of distinguishing between having your CPD done to you and instead taking ownership of it suggests to me that maybe part of what you're suggesting requires the creation of teacher researchers, who could be trained up by their HE institution. They could be the CPD specialists – if you like – within the schools who would actually be both a school teacher and in some sense linked to the university. You could actually reduce the amounts of work that you would have to do by just training up these people as researchers, researchers for the project, so the project would actually be very much a 'teacher-led but managed by us' kind of project.

A: I've got to say that what was in my mind was working with people who already have experience in a research role or professional development role in schools. The idea of partnership, I think is a good one and extending the ITT partnership into CPD and research because that's how I see it going. Many ITE partnerships are much more HE-led, that's true, but still there's still a lot of activity from schools.

P: Yes, so what's started out as a possible large scale funded project has now become something we could manage without any funding really, except our time. I suppose time is a resource; it has to be counted as money. So how big is it going to go before it becomes unmanageable by us?

A: What you could do is a very quick pilot project that could then enable you to write an informed bid based on data, some ideas that you've developed. So let's concentrate on no more than two clusters over a short period of time. Our objectives would be to identify CPD needs within those clusters and what possibilities could be for trying out new ideas to connect school-based CPD to HE CPD.

A basic question for any project is what its scale should be and this is one that you will have to address from the outset. As you can see from the discussion, the original very large-scale project has now come to be something much more manageable.

The next problem to deal with is one of *time*.

Illustration: time

P: If we just look at the pilot for a moment. The timing is quite critical because of the school timetable. We're now in February. We couldn't set this up for March because of Easter. But if we go into the summer, we interfere with exams in secondary schools and also SATS in primary, so that means that we couldn't do the pilot until September? Is that right?

A: I think so. Certainly we couldn't do it at the beginning of September. It would have to be at the end of September because people, including ourselves(!) have got to get into classes and get settled, but it does give you some planning time.

O: Yes I was going to say planning would take at least that long.

A: It does give you time to do a bit of a literature review, and to do some drafts of what it might look like, and talk to schools about it. So even though officially the pilot wouldn't start until much later, we would be talking to schools and doing things on the ground before then.

P: Yes. So staying with that timeline that, as you say, gives you plenty of planning time, we could presumably pull in the appropriate teachers to join the planning team for the pilot.

A: Yes, so it's a year from now that we'd actually work through to the larger project.

Sorting out a *timeline* (that is, a structure for the project, beginning with the first meeting and ending with the report, dissertation or whatever) is obviously important. Perhaps even more important is making it a realistic one so that it can be kept to.

A *literature search* has been mentioned in passing, but now some problems that such reviews have are discussed.

Illustration: literature search

P: Can I ask you a question, which is you mentioned doing a literature review. Would this be more than just library work? If so how would you carry that out? How would you actually look for research projects and so on that might be relevant to the research, that you know are running somewhere if you didn't happen to know that they were running?

A: Well, one of the ways of doing that is to look at conference proceedings because often conferences are where people present important projects in progress. So for instance the British Education Research Association papers, are online – you go there and have a quick look though to see what there was and you would come up with quite a number from last year's conference and if you do that internationally, you would perhaps be able to pick up quite a few other ones.

O: If you look at the DfES website to see what projects have been funded recently, you can see which ones are relevant and I suppose you could do that with the professional associations too.

P: The quick way into those associations is through the UCET website because they have links to other teacher education, or education-type research websites as well as DFES, TTA, GTC and so on. The UCET website is just 'www.ucet.ac.uk'.

O: But I think you've hit on an incredibly big problem for us let alone school teachers. There is just too much information.

P: I think that's why I paused there because ten years ago, even less, you'd think of researchers as going to the library, finding the most recent journal, looking at the biographies for the areas that you're interested in, and then following these up so you get the key references that are being used in relevant publications. That wouldn't work now, except as a very crude beginning.

A: I think as well, because people usually are involved in some kind of network or other, maybe it's not the partnership network, it might be through national scholarship, or school leadership – you have a range of people that you can actually talk to and find out what's going on and get contacts, people to ring or websites to look at, or whatever, because there are a lot of projects around and there are a lot of them that are producing newsletters, things like that, which are often on the web as well so it's spending time doing that and finding out.

P: So literature searches could be a virtual search, at least to begin with. You have got to find the key websites to go to get yourself off the ground. My last book I co-authored with Anne Edwards and David Hartley – they bring a psychological set of networks and a sociological set respectively to my philosophical ones and they had references which were directly relevant to my work, which I would never otherwise have identified because they had the kind of subject specialist background that they did. I guess if we were to work together, we might find the same, but not necessarily the same subjects but the networks that we constantly refer to, to formulate our ideas.

A: But increasingly, well especially with this particular idea about both, investigating, identifying and if you like accrediting school-based professional development, there's very little written about it. Generally speaking the professional development has been linked to something like being a teacher researcher, or it's been within a project or going on a master's course, or being part of some kind of initiative like the Literacy Strategy and Numeracy Strategy, which is concentrated on the content and the input, whereas what we're looking at here is teachers working together, teachers, if you like, coaching each other, teachers providing their own professional development or others with colleagues. This sort of topic is more under-researched than many other topics that you might want to look at, so we might have trouble finding appropriate literature.

O: I like the idea of a more collaborative emphasis, because the processes I think are still as important whether you're a lone researcher or whether you're a member of an action group or member of a staff group. Take for instance the network learning community that I'm working with at the moment – this is about raising achievement at the transition from Key Stage 1 to Key Stage 2, so they're concentrating a lot of their activity around that, in particular, new approaches to literacy development using media, film, digital film, all sorts of things, in trying to . . . [reach] the reluctant readers and writers. So right across 10 schools, you've got people collaborating and within those schools they're identified lead learners which is, I think, the normal thing that they're doing in there, 20 lead learners, two in each school, all of them have different, if you like, interests, they've all worked around a very broad theme, but all of them have different interests. They tend to work in pairs the two of them in the same school, and you've got there 20 teachers working around 10 themes under a broad raising achievement transition. So it's matching the school improvement agenda, as well as people's interests – because one of them's particularly interested in the use of video, one in particularly making films, story board-type of approach.

P: So we've got a project with a pilot, a rough timeline, we've raised a number of issues about the nature of research itself and what this does to the top down model with one of us at the top and the teacher at the bottom, or maybe the other way round, and there's this problem about the literature search nowadays not being as straightforward as it was. So you're looking for key websites really, as well as a good library.

Having established some of the problems of a literature search on a topic that has very little literature, the discussion then turns to the *questions to identify objectives* that the research will be dealing with.

Illustration: questions to identify objectives

A: Now I think one of the things we need to do is to really think in a bit more depth what the project would look like, what questions you would be asking, what kind of outcomes are we expecting and how are we going to do it. Because we seem to have a purpose – to provide, if you like, a pilot and an example of accrediting school-based professional development. So that's the kind of general idea isn't it? So what sort of questions do we want to be asking around that general idea? *How* are we going to do it first, rather than *what* questions? We're going to have some cluster groups of schools.

P: Well, we could do it that way. I wonder whether, if you take that idea I mentioned earlier, of having trained researchers implanted within the school, who are themselves schoolteachers – I mean, they're there already – what you would have is not so much clusters of schools but a group of schools that had people like us in them. Or at least people with the same thoughts that we have. It's rather like getting inexpensive research associates. One of the benefits for the people involved, bearing in mind you wouldn't expect them to have a career as professional researchers, is that the work would be part of their professional development. So it would be an example of professional development for them and of course for ourselves. But as you say, what we need are a set of objectives or problems that the project is supposed to address. Perhaps the first one is: what currently exists in the form of CPD?

A: And that's, I think, a really interesting one because if we look at what we found out from the sections of the CPD project and if I cast my mind back to 10 years ago, working with teachers, one of the biggest problems is identifying what professional development *is*. And also there is so much going on out there – do you want to acredit everything, or is there a sense of teachers deciding to select what to focus on in any one year, which links it very much to what's going on in each of the individual schools? So, yes, mapping the area, finding out what's going on and identifying what is termed 'professional development is your first step.'

O: And also more than that really in the political context that we're in, a national context, you've got to think of what is the current DfES model of professional development? Because ....al s a big issue, particularly since most of the teachers – three quarters of the teachers – have a very traditional perception of CPD and yet I think the government perception of CPD has moved right to the far end of it into peer coaching, lesson observation.

P: Teachers could appear to be trapped in their profession and so we could work through a model where you first become a teacher, then work through some form of CPD, which'll a'low you if necessary to move out of school teaching onto some other form of teaching. But now, the model that the TTA has of advanced teachers, SEN specialists and so on, are always in the school, there's little or no movement out of the school possible. The different funding regimes in universities as well makes it even more difficult to move out financially. So we've got a kind of CPD, which is narrowing the horizons rather than broadening them, and our project might be seen as trying to reverse that view.

A: There is also a feeling from government that every teacher should be involved in professional development of some sort. There is that feeling that CPD is not quite an entitlement and not quite a requirement. Whereas it was much more common 15 years ago for some people to say, 'Well I'm not interested in CPD, I'm getting on with my job'. And I suppose it was an understandable view, because there was a lack of recognition as to what was going on in terms of development in schools anyway.

O: And now the national initiatives have a CPD done *to* you, feel such as the national numeracy strategies of literacy, science Key Stage 3 strategy, and so on.

P: Yes, and TTA inset although it provides funding for CPD, you don't have any choice about it, you have to draw from a range of courses that are identified for you by the TTA.

O: What it's also doing coming back to your point, that a classroom focus doesn't allow you to look back at the ideology of the situation you are in, keeping you technically focused on what's going on. So having problems in the classroom doesn't allow you to question the literacy strategy, for example, that might be causing some of those problems.

P: It's interesting that because what you're describing is a form of centrist, TTA centrist CPD which first of all restricts the skills that you have and secondly prevents you being critical, so that CPD becomes a form of retention, a policy for retention, so it helps resolve one of the problems the TTA were having of retaining teachers professionally. This is very much a live issue. I think it's well worth following through.

A: It also raises for me the issue that teachers who are not involved in any sort of CPD activities, and the whole business of the assessment of prior experiential learning, which is something which happens anyway, in the majority of certificated courses. What I had been envisaging for a project like the one we're talking about, would ease and help people to identify more the experiential learning that takes part in the workplace. And therefore if they wanted to, it would also facilitate bringing that forward as evidence for certificated learning. It actually just accredits it and recognises it, and in that way charts a lot more what is actually happening on the ground of professional development, more so than what's happening at the moment. I do think one of the things that might be quite useful for us to do is to think about what we actually know about what's happening out there and to help us formulate questions. Because when I was thinking about this earlier, that having someone who is responsible for managing and organising professional development in this school is a good idea – many secondary schools already do have somebody, usually in the senior management team, but I can't say that that's true for primary schools. So my idea was that they would be the personnel we'd want to target first in this kind of project, as well as the head teacher, or somebody in the senior management team. So that immediately, as soon as you start approaching schools who want to be involved or could be involved, you go straight to the senior management team. The other implication is that it has to be a whole school thing, so therefore you have to concern yourselves with the management of the school. But the person who manages CPD, and the knowledge, and information that they need is key to what happens in the school. So that's where I would probably want to start by thinking about that person and how we could get them on board.

P: Yes. That would fit nicely with the pilot as well, wouldn't it? You could start to see whether that was possible with the pilot. So we've got a beginning of a structure, a kind of pre-history of CPD, immediate history of CPD, and then what exists now, so you contextualise the situation now, using history. We can do that from our own experience and publications. So that is quite straightforward, that section, rather like a standard dissertation – at least the first two bits – contextualising via a standard literature review. We might then need an interview or two with someone from the DFES or someone like Mary Russell or from the CPD committee at UCET, but we'd tidy that up quite quickly. That would then start to throw up questions, wouldn't it, that's what a good contextualising section does. As we've been doing today, you start to veer off in other directions, and get pulled back to the topic that you're supposed to be working on.

A: And there is a problem about evidence of prior learning, even when you consider a reflective journal, because if you look at things like performance management, and you look at what pupils do in terms of records of achievement I mean they're basically not worth the paper they're written on, people don't look at them, do they? You go for an interview and its like, oh yes, you've got a record of achievement. I think there's too much emphasis on written evidence anyway, and I wouldn't want to be going down the road of increasing teachers' workload by asking them to do even more. So we'd have to be thinking about what is worthy of credit and how you measure it.

P: It'd be interesting if we had as part of our team these small group of teachers who were these teacher researchers for the project, because we could ask them that question. What would they consider to be worthy of credit? Because they'll have degrees, some of them might have master's degrees. In fact by being part of the team they could join immediately the master's programme if they hadn't already got a master's degree, a master's by research. So perhaps we should be running concurrently with the project a master's research programme, just on research.

So it looks as if we've got the rough idea for a project fairly well planned out, the skeleton of it, and a clear topic. We're also saying we can't identify the key questions until we've done the contextualisation. We still need obviously to work out a more detailed timescale for the research.

So here you see that the further development of a research topic needs to be informed by the literature search, which provides a context within which it has meaning and a purpose. At this point in the discussion the three contributors then asked themselves how they came to identify a particular project they eventually worked up. What is interesting here is the way in which the examples given came from actual teaching situations which sparked an interest in taking the problems and puzzles that were thrown up further.

Individual ways of approaching research

Illustration: approaching research

P: What we've just looked at is a group of three of us looking at a project, which is going to be quite large scale, and requires funding, and preparation that goes with it. How about examining examples of our own research interests? I could draw on one that I had a while ago. There was a time when I got very very interested in IT, and its use in primary schools. And it came about because I was in primary schools watching people working, and I couldn't understand why they weren't using IT for the particular work they were doing. They were trying to design a newsletter for parents, but written by the children, semi-edited by the teacher concerned, but they were doing the whole thing manually. It struck me as bizarre because there were PCs along the corridor and they were just not using them. So I was faced with an issue there, why are they not using the equipment they could be using to do what they were doing? And that led me into talking with the teachers involved, and the children. The older children were also somewhat puzzled because they had IT at home. This led me to begin to write up this issue of what was happening to the IT policy that the then Conservative government was pushing in to the schools, to see what was going on. So I was looking at one school in my immediate area, which happened to have one of my children in as well. It was a highly personal situation, but it was possible to generate at least one research paper out of that. Now that's how I did it, it came out of a very personal interest, and also bumping up against the particular problem in a school. So how would you deal with a particular and personal research issue?

A: Well, I've done very little research totally by myself, but when I think about what I have done, it's been mainly practitioner-orientated because that's what drives me, as a researcher. So research either for a research degree or in terms of improving my own practice, and looking at how I worked with people, is how I would approach it, and that would probably be through some kind of reflective diary to start with, to try and get some ideas down on paper, and then actually monitoring and researching those ideas over a short period of time to try and look at how I would improve my practice.

One of the other things I've been doing recently which is slightly different, because I've been involved with quite a lot of empirically based research projects, is to use some of my experiences in that, to write a more conceptual piece about more ideas or policy rather than collecting data and researching in that particular way, which I've got to say I do find quite difficult! Recently I've just written a couple of pieces like that, and in a way, my inaugural lecture was kind of working towards that, it was based on projects that I'd done but I wasn't particularly reporting them. The lecture allowed me to do a little bit of reporting on data that had been collected. But really developing ideas, and particularly ideas about professional development, and in some ways I find that quite interesting to do, and I can do that by myself. And it involves quite a bit of re-doing, obviously, a lot of discussion, and a lot of reflective thinking, looking back, trying to make sense of what's happened in the past. So that's how I can try to approach it.

O: I haven't been involved in any personal research of this nature at all. As it happens all my research has been driven by funding, albeit I've become very interested in it afterwards, but it's been a very eclectic bunch and it's just been based really on what turns up and what liaisons I make. But a huge amount of it has been based on networks with the local authority advisers etc., and working with people and mainly it's been researching development projects. So really it's been almost exclusively looking at baseline research to see classically what the situation is now with a notion of implementing a new policy and then evaluating the new developments, whatever they are.

By and large it's always been with networks of schools and specifically with the teacher researchers in each network of schools, so I think about at least four if not five projects I've done have been based on that kind of model, which has thrown up issues of ownership which has always been a very key area that I'm very aware of.

A: What about your doctoral study though?

O: Yes, in fact I was thinking when you were talking about that – well I wouldn't call it philosophical in Peter's presence! But it was kind of deeply theoretical and literature based. Bits of it were empirically based and that was videoing my own practice, but I wouldn't lay claim to it being research. I wouldn't lay claim to doing any research until after I got my PhD.

Concluding remarks

Illustration: coming to a conclusion

A: In a way, partly what we're doing in the book is providing just that for practitioners. It's the basis of what we as experienced people working with teachers think that teachers need, in terms of research training, and ideas for doing research either alone or with groups.

P: It's interesting how very different that is because what we've just been talking about [individual research projects] doesn't require money, it just requires our time, so it requires manipulating your time if you were a school teacher again in the school to give yourself the freedom to do the PhD or whatever. I mean in my case, I actually took time out of school as a full-time teacher to get a master's degree, and became a supply teacher, so that I could control the amount of time I was working and the amount of time I was doing my master's degree. But that's only possible if you haven't got a family, and a house, and all the other responsibilities we tend to collect. Research does require a resource, time. With the large project what you're looking at is capital to allow you to do the project, in an individual project you're looking at time, which is the capital, to allow you to do whatever the project is. So it's the same principle, it's just on a different scale.

A: But we're different from teachers in school because (a) we're more experienced and doing research and (b) because in some ways it's a requirement of our job, to actually undertake some research, and we feel we've got something we want to say, and we want to make it public, whereas I think that some teachers find that aspect of it difficult because they've not been in a community, they've not been in an environment that actually supports such thinking. Teachers might talk about their practice, but it's difficult actually to talk about how you research it, or to say, 'Well I've been doing this, I've been investigating my practice and I think it might be quite useful if I talk to you about this'. So what's important is providing that kind of environment for teachers to grow in. Some schools have it, but it's giving teachers the confidence as well to be able to talk, and not just in a bland way, but actually to give detail in depth and rigour to the kind of work that's going on in the classrooms, and they don't always see the need to do it.

O: And we've also got to see what's driving a teacher to consider carrying out research. Let's face it where the money is for teachers is in things like advanced skills teachers whose salary can go up to £40,000. Now, what kind of CPD experiences would necessarily fit them for a kind of position like that because we're thinking of us wanting master's/PhD's? I can't begin to imagine that it's a PhD that would maybe get them along that route.

A: But I think there is a case for advanced skills teachers undertaking research themselves, and undertaking quite a bit of professional development, because they are in that kind of mentoring role with other teachers, and demonstrating a modelling role. So in some ways there're a number of things in terms of the subject knowledge in whatever area they're working in, that they do need to be in the forefront of, as well a the kind of skills needed to be working alongside somebody.

O: Mentoring I think is a key thing to a lot of the models of CPD that are around at the moment.

A: But you see this is where you need a community to debate things, especially while the pressure is on schools to conform to whatever strategy you've got to work with now, or whatever the flavour of the month is. It's interesting to watch emotional intelligence and accelerated learning and what have you, take over from literacy, because the nature of that is much more exploratory, at least you think it would be, but yet it's been presented as a package called 'emotional intelligence', a package called 'accelerated learning'. I think that's what teachers as researchers should be doing, making problematic and criticising the packages rather than accepting them. And I think there are people who are trying to do that, you just need to give them a voice.

P: I think that distinction (between the touchy-feely approach and everything's working fine approach, and the highly critical approach) is what we're trying to capture in the book aren't we? We're arguing that there's no point in the former, it's the latter which identifies a good researcher, finding appropriately critical evidence to substantiate whatever judgements you're making.

A: But often it's difficult to do that on your own. Even people like ourselves, professional researchers, don't always find the time to talk about an issue with other people. Do we always have colleagues asking questions making you rethink what you've been thinking? Like teachers we always ask, 'Is there time? Is there time to do it?'

5 Finding, Reviewing and Managing Literature

OVERVIEW

In this chapter we discuss the contribution that literature can make to your research. We begin by looking at different forms of literature that may inform your study, including materials relating to previous research in the area, methodology texts, readings about educational theory and philosophical or literary works. We outline some of the strategies that will be useful to you in searching for this literature in books, journals and electronic resources. We give you suggestions about how to establish a personal recording system and advice on formatting references in your bibliography and citing them in the text. Finally, we discuss briefly about how you should go about reading, reviewing and summarising the literature you eventually locate.

Types of literature

Before we start looking in detail at literature search strategies it would be helpful to discuss briefly the kinds of literature that may be of use to you in your research. First, reports of other research projects will be an invaluable source to build on. Ideally, you will have located and read some of these before you formulated the detailed plans for your study, and decided upon your research questions and methodology. There is a vast amount of research available, ranging from large-scale surveys to small-scale classroom-based action research inquiries; ideally it will be useful for you to explore studies of both these types. Locating relevant studies is not always easy but it is important, and later in the chapter we will give you some pointers as to where you may begin to look. You will want to be guided by previous research in the area, the methods they used, problems they encountered and the suggestions they may well have made for further research. The reason for this is not simply to avoid 'reinventing the wheel'. Indeed, in research it is often valuable to do exactly that – to replicate a research study in another context – and one criticism of educational research is that it rarely does carry out replication studies. Much useful information can be gleaned from comparing the findings of research studies, assuming the methodology is sufficiently well documented to be able to do so. A criticism not infrequently made, certainly in relation to educational research, is precisely that it is too fragmented and does not build cumulatively upon past studies, and/or test out current knowledge and understandings.

The second kind of literature you will need to consult will be methodological texts, or professionally focused research user guides, such as this one. They will give you practical ideas and support relating to your research. It is likely that you will need advice on how to go about identifying and refining your research area, defining research questions, and devising, planning and conducting your project. One of the most challenging decisions you will have to make, for example, is deciding upon the appropriate research method(s) to use. Short overviews, like the one presented in Chapter 6 of this book, are a useful introduction to the range of options open to you but you may well need to consult a book, or chapter in a book, relating specifically to the method you are intending to employ. There are a number of accessible texts of this nature suggested in the further reading section of Chapter 6 but if you are considering a non-standard data collection method, such as image-based research, for example, you will have to do a literature search to locate a relevant text. Data analysis is another important topic in which it is useful to have ideas from a variety of sources and a few are suggested at the end of Chapters 8 and 9, but again you may need to go into the specialist literature if your research methodology is non-standard. You will need to refer to such methodological literature not only before you commence your research but also at frequent intervals during the process.

The third literature domain you may well refer to embraces literature about education theory and practice relating to your area of interest. This might include ideological 'think pieces', books relating to pedagogy, official documents laying out educational policy, critiques of educational policy and so on. Such accounts will perhaps argue the case for particular policies or practices or relate sociological or psychological theories to the educational context. These will be important to inform your understanding of the issues surrounding the area of your investigation. They will also be effective as a source against which to bounce your own ideas, helping you to sharpen your debate or provoking you to produce counter-arguments.

Finally, there is a whole range of literary works, philosophical and historical writings, television and films that can be a great source of ideas. This latter category is most likely to be one that you will not expressly seek out; it is more probable that it is one that you will bring with you from previous reading and experiences. You will find that your memory will be jogged by particular events at certain points in the research process. Alternatively, current events or discussion with colleagues or your critical community may furnish you with information or spark ideas and suggest associations in previously unexplored territories. Such connections may add to the theoretical argument, provide insight to the analytical process, illuminate the analytical frame or simply enliven the writing up.

Managing literature

In our experience many, if not most, people embarking upon research for the first time begin their literature searches in a somewhat haphazard fashion. They start with one or two key texts and perhaps explore a number of others that are referenced in the articles or books ... and so their bibliography gradually grows. This method is certainly not to be dismissed and, indeed, the bibliography of a good review article is one of the best sources of further literature. However, the danger of adopting this rather haphazard generative method is that the small collection of papers that you once knew intimately will soon grow to such a size that you no longer know which book you found a particular quote or idea in, let alone which chapter or page number. Additionally, depending on your area of study, a systematic literature search will most probably eventually be necessary.

We cannot stress too much how vital it is that you devise your literature management systems before you embark upon searching for and acquiring literature. You must settle on two matters: the reference system you will use; and the method by which you will record the literature you have amassed and the key messages it contains.

REFERENCING SYSTEM

Dealing with the first of these matters, you will need to adopt a standard bibliographic referencing system. If you are enrolled upon an award-bearing course then you will most probably have had a standard system recommended to you; if you are not, then simply decide upon one of the standard systems and stick to it.

We recommend the Harvard System, which we use in this book, for referencing literature in the bibliography and citing it in the text. Harvard is a fairly standard system used by many publishers. It happens to be the one that is very attractive to authors as it allows you to give the bare minimum of information in the main body of your work, rather than having to give full details of a reference in, for example, a footnote which then has to be repeated in the bibliography. You will find that our 'resources for research' give you, through a straightforward question-and-answer session, a detailed breakdown of the formats you will need to use for authored books, chapters in edited books, journal articles, reports and web-published literature. The resources are organised to give you one example under each of these classifications but, when you construct the bibliography as a whole, of course, all these different types of literature will be arranged in one alphabetical list (see, for example, our own references).

PERSONAL INDEX SYSTEM

Having decided upon the reference system the next matter to attend to is devising an effective method which will allow you to record information about the books, articles and reports you read. We cannot stress enough how important it is to get this in place before you start to read and review this literature. Bearing in mind the bibliographic information you will require and details you will need for your own purposes (key words, quotes, synopses, etc.), we suggest the following format as a basic framework for an index system. You can use it as a blueprint and add to and personalise it as appropriate.

If the reference is of a book you will need to record the following details.

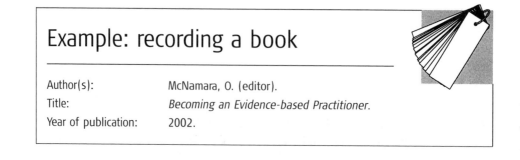

Example: recording a book

Author(s):	McNamara, O. (editor).
Title:	*Becoming an Evidence-based Practitioner.*
Year of publication:	2002.

Publisher's name:	RoutledgeFalmer.
Place of publication:	London.
Key words:	Evidence-based practice, partnership, practitioner research, case studies.
Points of interest:	Eight case studies written by teachers about their experience of researching in their own classrooms – includes methodological insights (*record page numbers*); chapter reflecting on partnership (pp. 155–71) . . .
Useful quotations:	'What counts as evidence? For whom is it intended? In what context is it to be employed? For what purpose is it to be used?' (*record page numbers*).

Where the book is an edited volume and you are particularly interested in one chapter you will need to record details not only of the book itself (as outlined above) but also details of the chapter.

Example: recording a chapter

Author(s):	McNamara, O. (editor).
Title:	*Becoming an Evidence-based Practitioner.*
Year of publication:	2002.
Publisher's name:	RoutledgeFalmer.
Place of publication:	London.
Chapter title	'One mouth, two ears: seeking ways to make children and teachers effective speakers and listeners'.
Chapter authors	Sarah Brealey and Claire Van-Es.
Chapter page nos.	pp. 79–89.
Key words:	Case study, video data, speaking and listening, primary phase.
Points of interest:	Use of video data to analyse strategies to improve the speaking and listening skills of children and teachers – Year 2, 3 and 6 (*record page numbers*).
Useful quotations:	'subjecting ourselves to the scrutiny of the video camera was painful but fruitful . . .' (p. 88).

For a journal article the minimum details you will need to record are as follows.

Example: recording a journal article

Author(s):	McNamara, O. and Corbin, B.
Title of article:	'Warranting practices: teachers embedding the National Numeracy Strategy'.
Title of journal:	*British Journal of Educational Studies.*
Year of publication:	2001.
Volume of publication:	49 no. 3.
Page numbers:	pp. 260–84.
Key words:	National Numeracy Strategy, evidence-based practice.
Points of interest:	Historical perspective on the introduction of evidence-based practice to education (pp. 261–2); analysis of ways in which teachers legitimated their professional judgements (pp. 270–8) . . .
Useful quotations:	See paper copy for highlighted text.

In the case of a journal article, the last two fields would perhaps be dealt with variably and we will consider this in more detail in the next section. If you have a paper copy of the article, and it is particularly rich with interest, you may well find it more useful to highlight possible quotations and interesting passages for future reference rather than copy or paraphrase them. A note to the effect that reference should be made to the paper copy could be entered in the index system (as above) and the paper copies filed elsewhere in alphabetical order, or perhaps catalogued.

It now remains to consider how to record this information. Such an index system is best recorded electronically but, if you do not have easy access to a computer, you can use a simple card index system to record the key fields. If you do have access to a computer then information such as references and quotations, once entered, can be cut and pasted easily into a bibliography or report.

There are a number of ways of managing the information you need to record on your computer. The simplest option is to use a word document in which individual entries are recorded alphabetically, as in a standard bibliography, and this would be quite adequate for the majority of small-scale practitioner inquiries. You could perhaps enter the information into a table organised in such a way that the columns contain the key fields and the rows are the individual entries. If you wished you could keep the entries in alphabetic form by inserting extra rows in the table at appropriate points. Whatever word document you construct for your particular purposes it can of course be searched using the normal 'find' facility.

An alternative option is to use a database such as Microsoft's Access, in which the fields recommended above can be set up and key-word searches completed, etc. There are purpose-made bibliographic software packages now available, such as End Note, which not only act as a customised database for referencing but can also be linked to compatible word-processing packages, such as Microsoft Word, to allow for references to be imported directly. End Note also has a facility to reformat and reorder references where necessary and, even more amazing, can import data electronically from certain national/international bibliographic databases and enter them directly into the correct field in the appropriate End Note library.

Searching for literature

Having established a system to document your literature, it is now time to consider how to find relevant texts. This will be best accomplished through a university library. Most practitioner researchers will be in some way associated with a university, through perhaps an Initial Teacher Training Partnership. Indeed, your study may perhaps be undertaken as one element of an award-bearing course, and you may have a considerable degree of support in devising the methodology and, perhaps, in selecting appropriate literature. Whatever your situation, if you are registered as a student at a university you will have full access to the university library and you should also be able to access the library catalogue and most of the associated electronic resources from your home. If you are not a registered student then just approach your local university, or the one you are most closely associated with; you will find that access is easier to negotiate nowadays than it used to be in the UK. If all else fails and you have a grant for your research, it may be possible to use some of the money in order to pay for access to the university library.

Libraries clearly vary but whatever contact you have, or negotiate, your chief point of access will be off-site through the library's web pages. There are now many services available that make libraries more user-friendly to off-site students including facilities such as electronic searches, document retrieval, borrower inquiries, loan renewals and reservations, etc. If you are a student on an award-bearing course you will undoubtedly have received a library induction when you enrolled, but the sheer volume of information you receive at this time makes it all too easy to forget, and the purpose of this section of the chapter is to remind you about the range of services that may be available. Although the detail provided here might not be sufficient to enable you to complete whatever transaction you require at your local library, it will at least alert you to the fact that such a facility may well be available so that you can make further inquiries.

In addition to the obvious final resort of browsing the appropriate sections of the library shelves, there are three main search domains available to you through the library: the main library catalogue, the journals catalogue and the electronic resources index. We will now briefly review of each of these domains, but do remember that the library will most probably have someone staffing an inquiry desk who will be only too pleased to help you with any queries or complex transactions.

THE MAIN LIBRARY CATALOGUE

Most main library catalogues will generally index reference and lending books, the audio-visual collection, master's/PhD theses and proceedings of annual conferences of research societies and similar professional associations. These items may be available for extended loan, short-term (usually overnight) or one-week loan or be available for reference and photocopying in the library only.

The main library catalogue will generally be searchable using various combinations of author/title/key word/topic search strategies. If you are looking for a particular text the more information you have on it the easier and quicker it will be to locate. If, as is more likely, you are looking for books on a particular topic then the search will be trickier, and you will need to experiment with search terms in order to narrow or widen the number of 'hits'. Having located a text, or texts, that appear interesting or useful you will need to note the library index number, but be alert to notice (and record in your own indexing system) whether items you have identified are on the main shelves, or perhaps in other collections. It may be that short-loan, audio-visual, reference, special, outsize or schools collections are stored separately. You will also normally be able to check the current availability of the items and place a reservation on a book if all copies are out on loan.

If you are unable to locate the book you require at your library you will be able to search the library catalogues of other libraries, and in particular the British Library, to which all UK university libraries have lending rights. An application through the Interlibrary Loan Scheme will enable you, for a small fee, to loan whatever book you require from the British Library. It will usually arrive within two to three weeks, but do ensure you return it on time as the overdue fee for such items can be considerable.

THE JOURNALS CATALOGUE

Much of the literature you will need to access, particularly the reports of research, will be located in articles in journals and to complete a systematic literature search you will need to explore their contents. All the journals held by the library will be catalogued in an index that will contain information such as the dates and volumes for which the journal is available. The catalogue will only list the titles of the journals and not their contents, so this is of limited value in itself, unless there is a particular journal or journals of direct interest to you. If this is the case then a good old-fashioned hand search of back copies might be worth resorting to at some stage.

The list of education journals is very extensive. There are, for example, subject-specific journals such as the *Journal of the National Association of Teachers of English* and special interest journals such as the *Journal of In-service Education* and the *Journal of Mentoring and Tutoring*. If your library subscribes to a journal in the specific area you are interested in then browsing back copies would be a profitable approach to locating useful articles. Adopting just this strategy, however, would not be sufficient; many authors publish in more wide-ranging areas of race, gender and disability and in general education journals such as the *British Journal of Education Research*, *Journal of Education for Teaching: International Research and Pedagogy*, *Journal of Teacher Education* and so on. Despite some journals preceding their title with 'American', 'Asian', 'Australian' or 'British' you should not be put off looking at those outside your own country's area, as authors publish in many different types of journal, irrespective of their country of origin. There is a way to locate articles on specific issues, however, without browsing the library shelves. This involves searching bibliographic databases and indexes and we shall return to discuss this below.

An enormously valuable growth area in relation to journals is the increase in the number of electronic journals now available and the rise in the number of publishers of paper journals that are making them available electronically. In practical terms this means that many of the journals in the library journals catalogue will have a link to the publisher's website and you will be able to access full-text versions of the journal directly. You will then be able to browse through the journals' contents pages, locate the volumes and part numbers of articles you require, download them and print them off in the comfort of your home.

An additional service that some publishers also extend to support awareness raising in respect of their titles is an alerting service whereby email alerts of contents pages of the new editions of journals are sent to anyone who requests them. The service can be accessed through the web pages of big publishing companies. The Taylor & Francis Group, for example, which includes publishers of a great many education journals, has a free alerting service called SARA (Scholarly Articles Research Alerting) to which you can subscribe. The British Library also provides electronic alerting services. Through ZETOC (http://zetoc.mimas.ac.uk), for example, you can access the Electronic Table of Contents of all current journals held by the British Library, and arrange for a personal alert to the table of contents of new issues of journals of your choosing. There are options on some alerting services to purchase the articles you require online but, beware, these services can work out very expensive and the Interlibrary Loan Scheme is a cheaper way to acquire such articles, as we will outline below.

ELECTRONIC RESOURCES

The growth in the volume, range and importance of electronic resources over the last five years has been awesome but, for a researcher, engaging with such electronic resources is an absolute must. However, not only is the scale of the enterprise overwhelming but the rate of change of the whole landscape is also alarmingly rapid – useful websites come and go, restructure and change addresses. Consequently, we will only mention a handful of the most secure web-based resources, each of which will have up-to-date links to other domains.

The whole gamut of sites which would be of interest to an educational researcher is very broad and includes newspapers (e.g. *The Times Educational Supplement*); institutions (e.g. universities, The British Library, NFER – National Foundation for Educational Research); organisations (e.g. BERA – British Educational Research Association, SCRE – Scottish Council for Educational Research, DfES, GTC –

General Teaching Council, UCET – Universities Council for the Education of Teachers); public and charitable foundations that fund research (e.g. ESRC – Economic and Social Research Council, Nuffield Foundation, Joseph Rowntree); and professional associations (e.g. NUT, NASUWT). There are also information gateways (e.g. SOSIG – The Social Science Information Gateway; NISS – National Information Systems and Services; BOPAS – British Official Publications Awareness Service; ePolitix – political awareness service); bibliographic databases and indexes (e.g. BIDS – Bath Information and Data Services; BEI – British Education Index); and electronic books and journals.

All the above electronic resources will be accessible via links available on a typical university library site, or go to the British Library site (http://www.bl.uk). Many of the sites are extremely valuable resources in themselves and it is difficult to select any out for particular reference. *The Times Educational Supplement* (http://www.tes.co.uk), for example, has not only electronic copies of the newspaper available but also archives of back copies, searchable by key word, title and date, and downloadable. ePolitix (http://www.epolitix.com/) has everything you could ever want about politics and politicians. The GTC England website (http://www.gtce.org.uk) has a Research of the Month page where current research is summarised in user-friendly form. The Teacher Training Agency has, amongst other research commissioned, published three sets of reports resulting from the Teacher Research Grant Scheme (1996–99), available not only in hard copy but also electronically, together with other research documents on the TTA website (http://www.canteach.gov.uk). The DfES website (http://www.dfes.gov.uk) has a collection of research briefs – four/five-page user-friendly summaries of the research studies they have commissioned. The briefs can be downloaded and printed. Likewise, some research funders such as the ESRC (http://www.esrc.ac.uk) and the Joseph Rowntree organisation (http://www.jrf.org.uk) have electronic databases of the research they fund, and reports and summaries can be downloaded. The Evidence for Policy and Practice Information (EPPI) Centre (http://eppi.ioe.ac.uk) was established by the UK government (*c.* 2000) to co-ordinate the commissioning and management of systematic reviews of educational research, and should become a very useful resource. NFER hosts a database funded jointly by EPPI and DfES of all Current Educational Research in the UK (CERUK) on their website (http://www.nfer.ac.uk). They also produce a research digest series called TOPIC, which is a collection of practitioner-friendly summaries of research published biannually, and may be available in your library, but check their website for further information.

There is clearly considerable variation in access arrangements to these sites but most are not password protected, which means that anyone can access them from anywhere. So, for example, if you were to go to a typical university, such as the Manchester Metropolitan University (MMU) (http://www.mmu.ac.uk), access the library home page and browse through the electronic resources you will discover that the greatest proportion require no password from within MMU or outside. It is becoming increasingly common for information gateways/hubs/databases, etc., that are password protected to manage their security and subscription arrangements through ATHENS (http://www.athens.ac.uk), the standard access management system for all UK higher education institutions (and much of the UK National Health Service). This has the advantage that you do not have to remember an armful of passwords but just an ATHENS ID and a username, which you will get from the library. This will secure access to most of the significant education electronic resources that are protected. You can use the account from the comfort of your own home.

BIBLIOGRAPHIC INDEXES AND DATABASES

Most important for our purposes amongst these many electronic resources are bibliographic databases/indexes. These are databases of journal articles only; they do not include reference to books or book chapters. Indeed, book chapters are the most intractable items to locate. Databases also have some remarkable gaps; the more esteemed databases in particular can be somewhat conservative in including new journals in their index. This is not normally a problem unless a journal vital for your area of interest is, for some reason, not included. For this reason it is important that you do not rely on just one search strategy – instead you should search perhaps a couple of bibliographic indexes and check for pertinent journals in the main library catalogue, perhaps sifting electronically through the table of contents of the past volumes.

In education in the UK, the main generic database is the British Education Index (BEI), which covers a very wide range of education journals from the academically prestigious to the professionally useful end of the range. BEI is an Anglicised version of the much more extensive and older US education index, ERIC. These two databases are extremely user-friendly and linked so that search strategies conducted in BEI can be transferred directly to ERIC and repeated. BEI and ERIC can be accessed through your local university website and through BIDS (http://

www.bids.ac.uk), which also has access to the International Bibliography of the Social Sciences and the Social Science Citation Index. BIDS requires an ATHENS password.

Search strategies for these databases vary, although again all are becoming a lot more user-friendly. As with general library catalogue searches you will have options of author(s), titles, key words in title and abstract and topic, etc. Some databases allow for simple searches (as above) or more advanced search strategies that allow for additional sophistication including years, languages, etc. Specific search terms/syntax are always explained in the help menu and include not only the usual AND/OR/NOT type of configuration but also useful truncations with wild cards (* or ?) which allow for a key word such as 'parent**' to locate items relating to parent, parents, parental, etc. Locating a manageable number of 'hits' (neither too few nor too many) is, of course, still a challenge. If you want to see just how challenging this can be try using the search term 'education' which, on its own, will produce so many 'hits' that you could spend many months following them up. Refining your search strategy in a broad research area such as education is obviously an absolute necessity.

You will probably require a few attempts at refining your search strategy by using different combinations of words, and perhaps combinations of previous searches, before you are satisfied that you have generated an acceptable number of hits. You have two options at this point: you can print or email yourself the entire list or, alternatively, you are generally offered the option to go through the details on screen to mark the ones you are particularly interested in. Once you have selected your 'marked list' you can then print the details off, or email them to yourself. You will be asked which fields to include in the emailed or printed report and it is important to choose an option that includes not only bibliographic details but also the abstract (if the article has one) and perhaps references (although these can sometimes be rather extensive).

When you receive your emailed and/or printed report go through the bibliographic details and abstracts carefully to consider which are of particular importance and prioritise them in a 'wish list'. Your next step is to check the journals catalogue of your university library to identify which of the articles are in journals available there. In the case of the ones that are you can simply go into the library and either read the article and make notes, or photocopy it and take it home (remember journals themselves cannot generally be loaned from the library). If an article you require is in a journal not held by your library then you can arrange for a photocopy of it to be sent to you through the Interlibrary Loan Scheme. This will again require the payment of a small fee to cover the photocopying and postage and receipt of the article may take a couple of weeks.

Reviewing your literature

The depth with which you read and summarise the literature you have now obtained will depend upon how central or useful it is to your area of study. Much of the literature will just require cursory attention. Indeed, for articles in particular, if you have acquired an abstract during the course of an electronic search, you may feel having read it that you do not need to obtain the full-text version. In the case of a research report you may be able to glean sufficient information relating to the methodology and findings from the abstract. So, for example, you may be able to report 'Evidencing pre and post tests Rain (1998) claimed that in a study of 152 trainee teachers 90% did not increase their subject knowledge during their PGCE' without reading more than a couple of lines!

It may be that other literature will warrant consideration that is more detailed. In order to help you decide whether a book is worth investing time and energy in, skim read the preface and introduction to get a sense of level and audience and you should find an overview of the structure of the book with perhaps a short paragraph on each chapter. If the book is an edited volume it will be much easier to identify useful chapters. In the case of an article, if you skim read the abstract, introduction and conclusion these will give you a fair idea as to whether the article should be read in more detail. If you feel it does not warrant further consideration – or the outlay of the cost of photocopying – just enter it in your personal recording system and make brief notes relating to what you have gleaned about the methodology and findings. Alternatively, just photocopy the abstract and conclusion. If you feel it does warrant further consideration then your approach to reading either an article or a book chapter would be best structured to a degree that goes beyond skim-reading, in order that you get the most out of what may well be a considerable investment of time and energy. Many research reports in particular are far from an easy read!

We will now consider how such a structured reading might be accomplished. If the literature in question is a research report then you need to pay particular attention to methodological issues, research methods used, how the sample was selected, the research questions posed, etc. Note any methodological weaknesses and importantly any themes for future research identified by the authors. If you have your own copy of the article or book chapter, highlight any passages that seem of particular relevance, or if not then make brief notes. If you are not able to enter the notes directly into your personal index system then remember to transfer the details as soon as you are able. Now move on to the research findings: what types of claim are made? Upon what evidence were they based? How was the data analysed? Was any attempt made to validate the findings by triangulating different sources of evidence? For example, were self-reported claims about professional behaviour made in interviews corroborated by observational data, or have they been left as rather subjective claims?

If the article or book chapter is a theoretical discussion, note down key words relating to the general focus, and a summary of the central thrust of the argument. Then on the hard copy of the article, if you have one, highlight section headings and passages where the author has made key points. So, for example, if they note that there are four reasons why a particular policy has failed to deliver the hoped-for improvements, highlight those reasons in the text, or note the essence of each of the points. Also highlight or record any especially outstanding sentences or short passages and in particular ones that say powerfully and succinctly what you would want to say.

We will come back to the topic of literature again in Chapter 10 where we think about the ways in which you might draw on the literature you have read and used in the design and execution of your research study when it comes to writing up accounts or reporting your research.

Further reading

Bell, J. (1999) *Doing your Research Project*. Buckingham: Open University Press.
This immensely popular research methods reader contains a number of useful chapters relating to finding, managing and reviewing literature: 'Keeping records, marking notes and locating libraries', 'Finding and searching information sources' and 'The literature review'.

6 Which Research Techniques to Use?

OVERVIEW

This chapter will suggest appropriate techniques to use in the research of professional development and practice. It identifies key questions for practitioners who wish to research their practice and reviews methods of reflective writing in diary, log and journal formats, biography, stories and critical writing approaches. There are also reviews of, and support for using, observation techniques, interviewing methods and schedules and questionnaires.

Research: what research?

Before suggesting which research techniques to use, it would seem appropriate to consider what kind of research is to be undertaken. The type of research undertaken by practitioners is usually small scale and focused on professional practice and thinking as manifested in the workplace. Practitioner research is often concerned with the improvement of practice, of teaching and learning and levels of care in medical and nursing practices. Research by practitioners is related to their everyday professional life and directly concerns their context or environment. It is affected by the prevailing social and political climate and is not uncontroversial. There are tensions and differences of opinions about what kinds of research matter and what kind of methods are appropriate for doing research. There is continuing debate about the value of practitioner research and applied research as opposed to 'pure' research.

This book promotes an approach that supports research aiming for the improvement of practice and has a commitment to practitioners themselves doing research into professional issues. It is important that practitioners have an understanding of the frameworks within which research has developed, especially the differences between scientific and interpretive research (see Chapter 1 for a fuller discussion of these issues). Similarly, the differences between qualitative and quantitative models of research are important aspects to consider (see Chapters 8 and 9).

Practitioner researchers can move along a continuum of methods when collecting data. Figure 6.1 is intended to indicate that there are degrees of structure within each method that determine the kind of approach researchers might take and would also influence the level of formality in the conduct of the research. As a result of the development of thinking and practice in practitioner and action research methodologies, there are no longer narrow, simplistic models of data collection and analysis. The 'myth' of systematic inquiry is also being questioned. Walford (1991: 1) refers to accounts of both scientific and interpretive research processes that show that, often, research is not neat and tidy. Rather it is: 'frequently not carefully planned in advance and conducted according to procedures, but often centres around compromises, short-cuts, hunches and serendipitous occurrences.'

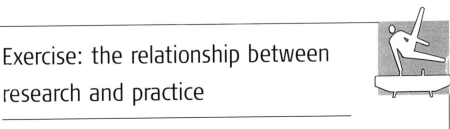

Exercise: the relationship between research and practice

Some questions surrounding the debates about the relationship between research and practice are given below in order to stimulate your discussion and thinking:

- ◆ Is it the role of practitioner research to provide 'tips' for practitioners?

- ◆ Is the goal of research primarily the development of more effective practices?

- ◆ Should research throw light on the socio-cultural processes that affect learning?

- ◆ Should all practitioner research demonstrate a commitment to reflect upon what happens in the workplace?

No one methodology dominates practitioner research and it is possible to be eclectic. However, issues of increasing importance are the justification for one's methodology, the consideration of ethical matters and the social context of research in the workplace. This last issue is particularly relevant to those researching the

Figure 6.1: INTERVIEWS

INFORMAL		FORMAL
Unstructured conversations	Semi-structured and loose schedule	Highly structured script

Observations

		Highly structured
Tape and video recording	Participant, non-participant	Time sampling
Diary/log		Checklist of items to be marked

Questionnaires

		Highly structured
Lots of room for individual responses		Closed questions and scales

INFORMAL

Unstructured

Open-ended – categories devised 'on the hoof'

Loosely structured

raising of achievement or the meeting of targets. A consideration of the rights and responsibilities of those participating in the research must be carefully undertaken in order to avoid discrimination and bias. However, it is difficult in social and educational research to isolate factors causing events or behaviour. Variables are not always easy to isolate in complex social and educational contexts where activities contain factors that interact and are interdependent. All the more reason, then, to have an over-arching, albeit flexible, structure for such research, which we identify as involving three stages.

Learning aid: structuring your research

The first stage to practitioner research design concerns the preparation and setting of questions or areas to focus on. Key questions are as follows:

◆ What to research?

◆ What are the aims of the research?

◆ Why do the research?

◆ How to do the research?

◆ Whom and when to research?

The second stage involves data collection. Again, there are key questions:

◆ What mix of data collection techniques and methods is to be used?

◆ When will the research take place and for how long?

◆ Where will the research be conducted?

The third stage is the analysis and evaluation of the data. Here the questions to be addressed include the following:

◆ Have the aims of the research been met?

◆ Was the analysis rigorous?

◆ Have the underlying assumptions been addressed?

◆ Have the data been evaluated?

◆ What are the implications of the research?

◆ What are the findings/conclusions of the research?

◆ How will the research be disseminated or made public?

This third stage will also involve consideration of a number of issues, including the following:

◆ Validity (do the conclusions follow from the arguments presented?).

◆ Reliability (are the methods used appropriate and relevant to the research aims?).

◆ Feasibility (were the research aims realistic?).

◆ Authenticity (is there a sense of reality about the research?).

◆ Representation (is the sample used appropriate?).

◆ Ethics (have issues of confidentiality and bias been considered?).

You need to make sure that these issues have been addressed to ensure that your research is robust.

When researching one's own practice or investigating aspects of professional development, some methods will be more appropriate than others. Small-scale research into one's practice is often open to criticisms of lack of objectivity and rigour. Qualitative methodologies are concerned with authenticity and voice and interpretations of situations and behaviour, and do not set out to 'prove' hypotheses in the same way as experimental, scientific research may do. This does not mean, however, that rigour, critical review and processes of checking validity do not form part of these small-scale research projects. What is generally called triangulation is frequently used to check the perceptions and interpretations of several people. Denzin (1970; 1985) distinguishes four types of triangulation:

1. methodological

2. investigator

3. theory

4. data.

Figure 6.2 gives more detail as to how to undertake the different types of triangulation. Involving colleagues is desirable, whether they are colleagues in school, those in your course group or colleagues you meet through action research networks or cluster groups of schools. Colleagues can be very useful to you as 'critical friends' or 'critical community' members. The cross-checking and the gathering of differing perceptions about research is an essential way of ensuring reliability and authenticity.

The concepts of critical friendship and critical community are discussed in detail in Chapter 7; however, brief descriptions of the role are presented here. A critical friend is someone who acts as a peer reviewer, asking questions in supportive yet challenging ways. It could be characterised as a kind of partnership in investigation of practice. A critical community extends the notion of critical friendship from an individual to a group of people acting as a way of debating and examining practitioner research. The community could operate in a variety of ways: as a sounding board; as a group of experts in the research area; or as a group of lay people who might represent those with a stake in the developments being undertaken by the researcher.

In the paragraphs that follow, a number of common and useful research techniques will be introduced and reviewed, as follows:

◆ Reflective writing, diaries, logs, journals.

◆ Biography, stories and fictional critical writing.

Figure 6.2: TRIANGULATION

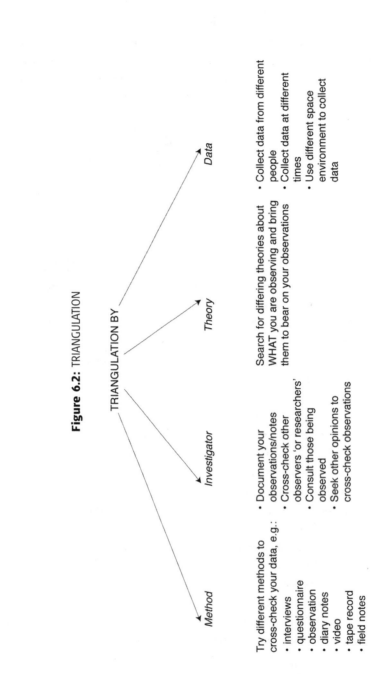

TRIANGULATION BY

Method	Investigator	Theory	Data

Try different methods to cross-check your data, e.g.:
· interviews
· questionnaire
· observation
· diary notes
· video
· tape record
· field notes

· Document your observations/notes
· Cross-check other observers 'or researchers' Consult those being observed
· Seek other opinions to cross-check observations

Search for differing theories about WHAT you are observing and bring them to bear on your observations

· Collect data from different people
· Collect data at different times
· Use different space environment to collect data

- Observation.

- Interviewing.

- Questionnaire design.

Reflective writing, diaries, logs and journals

Many writers feel giving a personal response to events and situations is a kind of therapy. Recording one's reactions and thoughts to events and situations, how one felt, how one behaved, can tap into the inner self and serve to develop understanding. This can be a very subjective account or perspective, but it can provide important insights into situations. It is important, however, to keep to a professional code when writing and to observe an ethical code that is non-discriminatory and which recognises the dilemmas which teachers face in the course of their professional lives. The guidelines produced by the British Educational Research Association (BERA – bera.ac.uk/guidelines.htm) are a very useful resource for identifying and resolving such dilemmas for researchers.

REFLECTIVE ACCOUNTS

Reflective writing is a major tool for a teacher researcher who wishes to investigate and research practice with a view to improving and refining his or her practice. Most teachers in schools today will have qualified through course models that espoused the development of the reflective practitioner at either initial teacher education or continuing professional development stages. Schön (1983) coined the phrase 'the reflective practitioner' which, according to Day (1999: 26), has become synonymous with good practice (see also our Chapter 1).

Currently there is much debate about the relationship between reflection and technical aspects of teaching. Our view is that having access to a 'technical toolkit' is not sufficient in itself to create or support good teaching or researching. Rather, one has to know why any particular strategy or method is appropriate at any given stage or time. This involves understanding frameworks or paradigms for teaching and researching.

Arguably, effective teachers and researchers ask good, well framed and probing questions and are good listeners and readers. In order to ask appropriate questions, it is necessary to have a conceptual framework on which to draw so as to know what is and is not appropriate. Eraut (1994: 124) offers a five-level model of teacher development that spans the territory from novice to expert and identifies reflective and analytical approaches at expert level. Day (1993) also reminds us that collaboration improves reflective practice and that reflection alone is not sufficient for the improvement of practice.

However, evaluating events by writing reflectively, and critically appraising the process and outcomes with other researchers or colleagues, can stimulate renewal and provide useful research data and indicate areas for further development. Some questions to address when starting to write a reflective account are as follows:

- ◆ What has been successful and why?

- ◆ Which strategies or approaches worked well? Why?

- ◆ What were the difficulties?

- ◆ What action can be identified to improve the situation in the future?

- ◆ What can I do? What can others do?

- ◆ Do I need an action plan?

- ◆ How will this be monitored?

DIARIES, LOGS AND JOURNALS

Practitioner researchers may also find it useful to keep a diary or journal. This document would be part of the data collection, and extracts or transcripts could be used or referenced in any report or account of research. Attention should be paid to confidentiality issues. The style of writing should be that of professional discourse, reflective and analytical, but using everyday language and professional terms. It is advisable not to identify particular institutions, colleagues or children but to use alphabetical or numerical notation when necessary (e.g. teacher X and child 5 in institution Y). There is currently some discussion about confidentiality issues that indicates that perhaps there should be an acknowledgement and celebration of successful practice and good practice by naming teachers and schools. Whatever, the consideration of, and discussion about, ethics and confidentiality issues is an important and essential part of doing research (see Chapter 10 for further discussion of ethical and confidentiality issues).

Some different ways of recording thought, actions and evidence are:

◆ critical incident analysis

◆ informal observation

◆ log of events.

Critical incident (or scenario) analysis is an interesting and innovative way of looking at the professional experience and life of practitioners in education and related professions. As part of keeping a diary, it may be useful to use a variety of approaches to help structure the writing. It involves a great deal of reflection on incidents and events that occur as part of one's professional life, and then selecting those incidents and dilemmas which are rich and which can be critically reviewed with a view to understanding and developing thinking and practice. The classic example is the impact of the window cleaner and his ladder upon a lesson. But there are hundreds more and they happen to practitioners all the time.

In some ways undertaking a critical incident analysis relies on the ability to analyse and appraise situations, which is helped by a researcher/teacher's abilities to focus on key incidents, events or situations that might yield data relating to the professional concern or research focus. Some questions that may aid the process are as follows:

◆ What led up to the event?

◆ What happened?

◆ What was the outcome?

◆ How would you take action from this critical incident?

◆ How can you make action judgements, diagnostic judgements, explanatory judgements, reflective judgements and critical judgements?

◆ How will you check out your perceptions of the events with another observer or participant?

For an in-depth look at critical incident analysis you should consult David Tripp (1993).

A log of events can quite simply be a list of events, dated and timed. Keeping a log can be useful in documenting your own behaviour or that of others. It could be a list of interactions of a particular type for analysis or a log of the different roles you undertake as a researcher. Logging the course and the conduct of the research project can also be a useful aid to writing up your methodology.

The terms log, diary and journal seem to be used interchangeably. Bolton (2001: 156) refers to the work of Holly (1989) in order to distinguish between them. A log seems to be characterised by its straightforwardness, like an *aide-mémoire*, being highly selective like a ship's log which would never claim to be a record of everything that occurred on board. A diary can 'contain anything' and 'be a confessor, a confidante, or a special friend . . . just like a reflective practitioner's writing' (Bolton, 2001: 157). A journal, however, is like a diary but includes 'deliberative thought and analysis related to practice' (Holly, 1988: 78).

It is important to consider the timing and frequency of diary/log/journal entries/ reflective accounts. As a rough guide, our experience of working with teacher researchers indicates the following time frames to be useful:

◆ *Critical incidents* should be recorded as and when they occur.

◆ *Informal participant* [*observation*] should be recorded when you have a set of questions to investigate.

◆ *Log of events* should be recorded daily or weekly if selected or specific events occur at that interval.

◆ *Personal response*: whenever the situation demands it and you feel 'moved' to write.

◆ *Reflective account* should be once or twice weekly for entries which review events and less frequently for non-specific reflection.

Biography, stories and fictional critical writing

Less well explained in the research literature is the use of biography, stories, pen-portraits and fictional writing. Nevertheless, teacher biography and teachers' stories are established methodologies (Ball and Goodson, 1985; Dadds, 1995; Thomas, 1995), but the fictionalisation of settings and characters is less well established. Campbell and Kane (1998) and Campbell (2000) have developed fictionalising research data in the investigation of school-based training drawing on the work of Winter (1985) and Clandinin and Connolly (1996). Pen-portraits, developed to illustrate and depict teachers' perceptions of professional development, were utilised by Hustler *et al.* (2003) in a major UK government-funded project which investigated teachers' perceptions of professional development. This involved amalgamating evidence gained through interview into teacher pen-portraits to depict common experiences and views about professional development.

Hardy (1986) called narrative 'a primary act of mind' and gave 'storying' a central place in logical thinking. Thomas (1995: xii), in his introduction to a collection of teachers' stories, notes that: 'story telling can be captured in logs, diaries, research journals, vignettes, life histories or autobiographies . . . can be seen as ways in which the person socially constructs him or herself' and refers to Woods (1993) as providing clear evidence of the value of personal narrative to the development of teachers and teaching.

Talking with teachers about their personal experience of teaching and constructing a life history give good insight into the profession, and these techniques would also apply usefully to other professions. Thomas (1995) provides a long list of the varieties of biography and story already in the literature, ranging from a newly qualified teacher (NQT) who was interviewed and observed closely by Bullough *et al.* (1991), to teachers of English writing their biographies (Beach, 1987), and a large-scale study of the professional and private careers of primary teachers (Nias, 1989).

Learning aid: writing a biography or telling a teacher story

Some methods, which might help in starting to write a biography or to tell a teacher story, are given below:

◆ Construct a simple *curriculum vitae* and then identify two or three major development or growth points or professional 'disasters', if appropriate, from each entry in order to begin a biography.

◆ Think of the most rewarding time in your career and start to unpick the reasons why and the events that led up to it.

◆ Write a short pen-portrait of yourself as a teacher. Pair with a colleague and each of you construct an informal interview schedule based on reading the pen-portrait which aims to engage in a professional dialogue about each other's career developments and history.

◆ Think of a particular difficult or amazing pupil or student from the past. How did you deal with this person? What key characteristics can you identify from your behaviour? How does this fit with your perceptions of yourself as a teacher?

◆ Interview pupils or students about your teaching. Care should be taken to elicit stories that are authentic, not just what the listener might want to hear.

It is not much of a step to begin to fictionalise the data collected from research or from teachers' writing above. Fictionalising data allows the writer to bring the voice of the participant to the centre of the stage and also allows for the amalgamation of 'real' stories and 'fictional' stories as exemplars for discussion and critique. Clandinin and Connolly (1995; 1996) talk of teachers' professional landscapes and believe that the access to those landscapes which will unlock professional development is best gained through story. As teachers tell and retell their stories, different versions are evident as new insights are gained and prevailing 'band-wagons' influence interpretations.

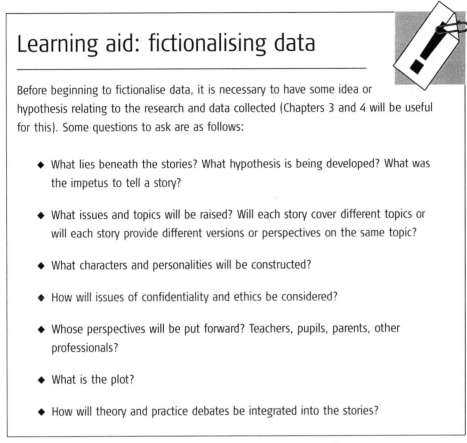

Learning aid: fictionalising data

Before beginning to fictionalise data, it is necessary to have some idea or hypothesis relating to the research and data collected (Chapters 3 and 4 will be useful for this). Some questions to ask are as follows:

- What lies beneath the stories? What hypothesis is being developed? What was the impetus to tell a story?

- What issues and topics will be raised? Will each story cover different topics or will each story provide different versions or perspectives on the same topic?

- What characters and personalities will be constructed?

- How will issues of confidentiality and ethics be considered?

- Whose perspectives will be put forward? Teachers, pupils, parents, other professionals?

- What is the plot?

- How will theory and practice debates be integrated into the stories?

The writing up of biographies, stories and fictional accounts is greatly dependent on the abilities of the writer and the ability, as in drama, to suspend disbelief. It is, however, an enjoyable and interesting approach to research. Examples of fictionalised accounts can be found in Campbell and Kane (1998), especially in the chapters dealing with student teachers' and mentors' perceptions of the challenges, trials and tribulations of school-based training. See chapters 8 and 10 for further support regarding the analysis of this type of data.

Observation

One approach to practitioner research is informal participant observation. Recording what you see as you participate in teaching or meetings or other educational events can provide evidence as to what is happening. 'Insiders' in events often understand the significance of what is happening as they are very much in tune with the context. On the other hand, because 'insiders' are very familiar with the day-to-day routine, it may be difficult to see anything 'new' in events.

Use can be made of time-sampling techniques (noting every so often at intervals of one minute onwards what is happening) or recording the frequency of events (recording every time a certain event or behaviour occurs). Just simply noticing events can also provide insight into situations.

Many researchers develop this technique as taking field notes. Taking field notes as part of research is a recognised and well developed research method, adapted from ethnographic and anthropological research for use in educational settings. Hitch-cock and Hughes (1989: 67) suggest that field notes can be contextualised by background notes and are often supplemented by gathering data by other methods, such as interviews or structured observations (that is, triangulation). It is useful to get into the habit of dating and timing your observations and reflections in order to use them as evidence and provide a system for organising them.

The issue of subjectivity is relevant to many qualitative and interpretive approaches. Macintyre (2000: 62) discusses the issues of selection of what to record and the need to maintain a professional code of practice when researching. As long as objectivity is not claimed in the research and that research methods are justified and critically reviewed, subjectivity is accepted and recognised as a perhaps inevitable feature of small-scale qualitative research. Thus Dadds (1995: 68), when discussing 'Vicky' the action researcher and her personal convictions and her personal presence in her research, claims that 'subjectivity enriched its authenticity'.

Making observations is far more complex than it sounds at first hearing, especially in professional situations such as the schoolroom as:

> classrooms are exceptionally busy places, so observers need to be on their toes. Every day in classrooms around the world billions of events take place: teachers ask children questions, new concepts are explained, pupils talk to each other, some of those who misbehave are reprimanded, others are ignored (Wragg, 1999: 2).

Observation has many uses in the various social and educational settings in which professionals in education and related fields find themselves. It is an integral part of human behaviour. We all make observations as we go about normal everyday life. Observing as a part of the process of doing research is different, being more organised around a specific focus, although some researchers use very open-ended and unstructured approaches.

Another complicating factor is that it is now much more common to find more than one person in each educational or workplace setting and for there to be collaborative work practices in classrooms and other settings. Observation of professionals at work is a more frequent phenomenon than in previous years: for inspection purposes, for training purposes and for assessment purposes. The kind of observations that are undertaken in a research context are systematic and organised to suit the aims of the research and the style of research. Types of observation can range from highly structured schedules to 'noticings', which are informal and happen incidentally.

We suggest that a few guidelines should be followed. First the purpose and focus of the observation must be decided, which will greatly influence the type of observation used. Some purposes might be to observe:

◆ pupil, teacher or student behaviour;

◆ teaching performance;

◆ pupil interaction in particular contexts;

◆ the nature of pupil–teacher interaction;

◆ the frequency of certain events; or

◆ the rating of behaviour or interactions.

Approaches to observation can be described as either quantitative or qualitative and are demonstrated by the continuum below:

$$\text{Pre-ordained} \longleftrightarrow \text{Open}$$

Observations of all types offer insights into situations and can often be combined in powerful ways to 'saturate' situations. Many research projects successfully combine quantitative or survey methods with qualitative or interpretive methods.

Quantitative observation is characterised by highly structured, systematic schedules. Rating scales, such as those devised by Likert, allow researchers to make judgements against defined criteria. An example of a behaviourally anchored rating scale is given below. It refers to the observation of pupils in a science activity using a five-point (Likert) rating scale.

Example: observing pupils in a science activity

1. = Pupil is fully engaged on task and fully occupied.

2. = Pupil is mostly engaged on task and is occupied.

3. = Pupil is frequently engaged on task and is occupied.

4. = Pupil is sometimes engaged on task and sometimes occupied.

5. = Pupil is seldom engaged on task and seldom occupied.

The use of opposite behaviour or mood characteristics can be used as a rating schedule.

Example: observation of teaching behaviour or characteristics

Informal	1	2	3	4	5	6	7	Formal
Lively	1	2	3	4	5	6	7	Dull
Eye contact	1	2	3	4	5	6	7	No eye contact

Wragg (1999: 23) identified some criticisms of rating scales, not least the possibility of differences between observers, their use and judgements in observation, although training of observers until they show high agreement with each other's systems may lessen these subjective differences. Simpson and Tuson (1995) refer to the valuable work of Powell (1985) in the development of the System for Classroom Observation of Teaching Strategies (SCOTS schedule) and of the selection of an appropriate rating scale. Obviously a great deal of time will be taken up with identifying the categories to be rated, with careful reference to the range of behaviours or features in the area to be researched being absolutely necessary.

Care should be taken to note when inference is being made by the observer, as the reader should know when this is happening (for example, does a nod mean that a person understands what has been said, or is he or she simply trying to appear as if he or she understands?). There is nothing wrong with using inference as long as it is recognised that that is what is happening and that value judgements might be being made by the observer. Two instances of how inference can be measured are given below.

Illustration: 'Pupil happily reads her book'

This observation requires considerable judgement by the observer and has a high inference as the judgement of 'happily' requires the observer to infer from his or her viewpoint what is meant by someone else's (the pupil's) body language and facial expressions.

Illustration: 'John used his handkerchief ten times in the mathematics session'

Low inference is evident in this observation as the observer is recording the recurrence of discrete pieces of behaviour.

Having a specific focus for observation inevitably structures the observation. It is necessary to highlight the different features in the context being researched. For instance, there will be a difference in what is being looked for in a modern foreign languages session with 15-year-olds and a story-time session with a nursery class. The quality of the analysis of the context will significantly affect the quality of the observation schedule design. Observation is not done in a vacuum. To neglect the details of time of year, size of classroom and learning environment in the description and setting for the observation leaves the reader in a disadvantaged position and would mean that questions could be posed about your research concerning factors such as validity, reliability and authenticity, identified earlier.

Interviewing

A frequently used research method is the interview, and in fact this is something we used in Chapter 4. There are many different types of interviews, ranging from highly structured, formal interviews to informal conversations (ours was semi-structured). You must choose the form to suit your purpose after carefully considering what style and approach to data collection you wish to pursue. For many practitioners interviewing colleagues, pupils or clients a more informal style is appropriate, though a structure of some sort is required.

Learning aid: interview planning

When you are making preparations for interviewing, consider the following:

◆ The setting for the interview in order to consider comfort, privacy and seating.

◆ Timing to suit interviewee and duration of interview. Remember that long rambling interviews are difficult to record and could be seen as a waste of time.

◆ A need for clarity of focus for the interviewee is essential in order to maximise the time and give a sense of value to the interviewee.

◆ How structured will the interview be? Consideration of what you want to achieve as a result of the interview should be clear in your mind at the outset.

◆ Planning of prompts, probes or follow-up questions. It is useful to have these prepared so that you don't 'dry up' or have nothing to say.

◆ Preplan the way you will analyse the interview so as to aid the process of interviewing. It is always useful to have some notion of the way you intend to analyse the material when interviewing.

◆ Whether to record the interview or not (recording does allow for more eye contact and focus on the questions to be asked). A negotiated (between the interviewer and respondent) account can be produced as the outcome of the interview which serves as a summary of the main points.

It would appear that many individuals feel pressure to want to give answers to interview questions that please the interviewer and many try to guess the answer favoured by the person asking the question. Some discussion at the beginning of an interview about feeling able to give an opinion could alleviate this pressure. Confidentiality must be assured if there is any risk or disadvantage to the interviewee or if the topic is controversial. There has been some discussion in the research community about whether anonymity is always the best solution to issues of confidentiality, there being some concerns that omitting the names of informants may result in practitioners' contributions to research in the workplace remaining hidden and unrecognised. Whatever is decided, again it may be useful to consult the Ethical Guidelines produced by the British Educational Research Association (BERA – www.bera.ac.uk/guidelines).

One major pitfall to avoid is asking predominantly 'closed' questions or questions that appear to have a factual or right answer such as 'Do you think research can be done in classrooms?' or 'Is it a good idea to base teachers' professional development activities in schools?' Both these could be answered with either 'Yes' or 'No' responses. Interviews should aim to be exploratory and facilitate the giving of information or opinions and be discursive in nature. Use open questions such as 'How would you describe your recent professional development activities?' or 'What kinds of activities do you think would best support you in your professional development?' Open-ended questions facilitate the giving of opinion and allow the respondents opportunities to develop their responses in ways which the interviewer might not have foreseen.

Most interviews will use a range of open and closed questions. The work of Hitchcock and Hughes (1989: 79–93), summarised below as types of interviews, may help to structure the format of any interviews planned.

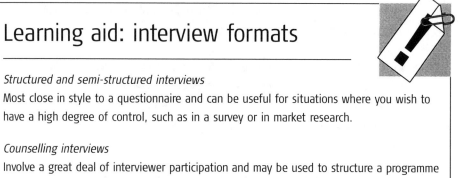

Learning aid: interview formats

Structured and semi-structured interviews
Most close in style to a questionnaire and can be useful for situations where you wish to have a high degree of control, such as in a survey or in market research.

Counselling interviews
Involve a great deal of interviewer participation and may be used to structure a programme of intervention or give advice to colleagues or pupils involved in reviewing their work or practice.

Diary interviews
Focus on reviewing diary entries and providing interpretations or explanations after the event. These could be useful in developing reflective evaluations of teaching and learning.

Life history interviews
Allow researchers to ask about the interviewees' personal, professional experiences in ways, that encourage anecdotal and narrative accounts of their lives in teaching.

Teachers' biography
A well documented methodology in researching professional development (see Ball and Goodson, 1985; Goodson, 1992; Thomas, 1995).

Oral history interviews
Provide opportunities for respondents to provide a historical account of the past in relation to information they may have or their memories of events and incidents.

Ethnographic interviews
Involve the researcher in working like an anthropologist. Studying a way of life takes account of the context, identity of persons involved and their relationship to each other, and the variety of social, cultural, institutional and linguistic factors influencing the interview. It is a naturalistic interview technique.

Telephone interviews
Sometimes used when dealing with people in remote places or who have difficulty finding time for an interview. There are limitations in telephone interviews due to the inability to see facial expressions and body language. Para-linguistic utterances, such as 'uh-uh', 'mmm' and 'um hum', can be used by the interviewer to encourage talk and support the interviewee.

Group interviews
Where one interviewer interviews several people may require tape recording, as note taking at the same time as guiding the discussion could be difficult. Alternatively, a 'scribe' can be used.

Unstructured interviews or conversations
Non-directive and offer greater scope for asking questions. Some attention to issues concerning systematic inquiry and validity is necessary. Many researchers find the informality of unstructured interviewing very suitable to 'insider' research contexts when working with colleagues or familiar pupils or clients.

Whatever type of interview is selected, interviewers must try to reduce bias, often by rehearsing (or piloting) the interview with a friend who can then give feedback on how the interviewer's views on the topic being researched are evident. After reflection further steps can then be taken to reduce any bias. It is always worth while to trial or pilot questions in the pursuit of high-quality data, which will result in interesting and worthwhile analyses. The quality of the questions asked will directly affect the type and quality of the responses. It is also a good idea to have well thought-out and preplanned, but not intrusive, strategies for probing interviewees.

In conclusion there are a number of useful tactics:

◆ Have a well prepared schedule.

◆ Be friendly but business like.

◆ Help interviewees to be explicit in their answers.

◆ Try not to lead your interviewee.

♦ Try to use verbal and non-verbal tactics to structure the interview, rather than leading or dominating it.

♦ Keep checking your approach and style by listening and reviewing your tapes and notes.

Analysing the data from interviews

There are many advantages in transcribing taped interviews, such as access to a complete account of the interview and the facility to scrutinise detail. But there is one major disadvantage, and that is time. For many readers engaged in small-scale research of their own and others' professional development, time or secretarial support will not be available. It may be useful to consider taping the interview and selecting short extracts for transcription and providing a negotiated account of the rest of the interview (for further, more detailed, advice on analysing data, see Chapter 8).

Using questionnaires

As with designing an interview, questionnaires need careful and detailed preparation if they are to yield a high quality of data: they are, in a sense, an interview without the presence of the interviewer. The quality of the questions asked will directly affect the quality of the data gathered. Hopkins (1993: 134) states that questionnaires provide a quick, easy way of accessing pupils' views of what happens in the classroom and can give specific detail about a teaching method or aspect of the curriculum. He also suggests that cartoon pictures make the completion of a questionnaire more fun. If the researchers are interested in pupil feedback about their teaching then developing simple, uncomplicated questionnaires which pupils are motivated to complete will be an advantage.

As with interviews, questionnaires may include closed and open questions depending on the data required. Open questions that allow for individual response will, of course, present more challenges in the analysis stage. One of the biggest problems with questionnaires is the low response rate (sometimes well below 20%), but perhaps if the researcher is well known to the respondents it may positively affect the response rate. One other disadvantage to questionnaires is the time-consuming nature of the design and analysis. However, questionnaires can yield specific information from a group of people in cost-effective ways.

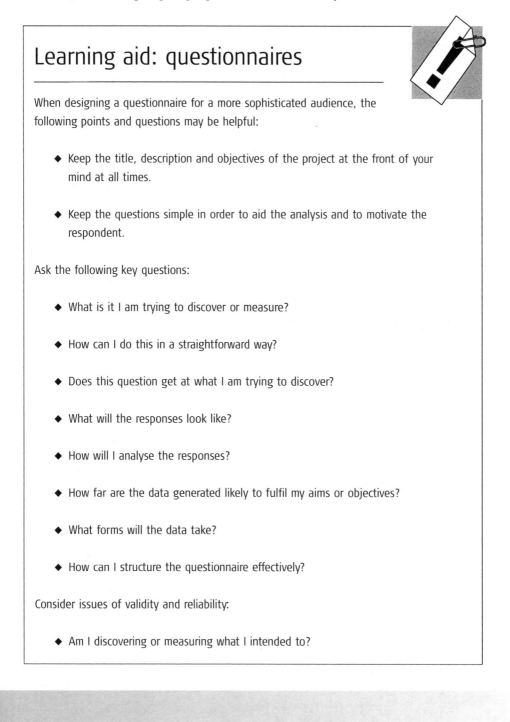

Learning aid: questionnaires

When designing a questionnaire for a more sophisticated audience, the following points and questions may be helpful:

◆ Keep the title, description and objectives of the project at the front of your mind at all times.

◆ Keep the questions simple in order to aid the analysis and to motivate the respondent.

Ask the following key questions:

◆ What is it I am trying to discover or measure?

◆ How can I do this in a straightforward way?

◆ Does this question get at what I am trying to discover?

◆ What will the responses look like?

◆ How will I analyse the responses?

◆ How far are the data generated likely to fulfil my aims or objectives?

◆ What forms will the data take?

◆ How can I structure the questionnaire effectively?

Consider issues of validity and reliability:

◆ Am I discovering or measuring what I intended to?

◆ Will the way I have worded the questions get a similar reaction from all respondents and at different times of administration?

Be aware of timing, structure and piloting issues:

◆ Use different sections, fonts and colours for different types of question/data.

◆ Will the questionnaire be able to be completed in an optimal time of five minutes?

◆ Are the explanations and instructions to respondents unambiguous, simple and clear?

◆ Do you need to promise confidentiality?

◆ Do you need to explain what will happen to the collected responses?

◆ Have you considered the analysis of the data as you construct the questionnaire?

◆ Have you asked anyone to review the questionnaire and offer a view on whether it is a good questionnaire?

◆ Have you undertaken a trial?

Be prepared to pilot the questionnaire on a small sample and be prepared to make changes.

Conclusions

It will be obvious that there is no shortage of research techniques for a practitioner researcher to employ. These are the most suitable methodologies to the field of practitioner research that relies to a great extent on day-to-day activity in a changing landscape. However, it remains our belief that practitioner research is essentially untidy. It lends itself to illuminative approaches, particularly in the context of monitoring and evaluation. It is for this reason, as will be discussed subsequently, that lively and engaging dissemination is critical. In order to allow us to make it possible for you to see clearly what the different techniques are and how you might, as a practitioner researcher, use them we have treated them in isolation from each other. Our last suggestion in this chapter is that, despite the way we have structured our material here, you should also be prepared to make use of a combination of techniques in order to produce as rich a data set as possible which can then inform your research of your practice.

Further reading

Bell, J. 1993) *Doing your Research Project*. Milton Keynes: Open University Press. This is a well-known and readable book for beginner researchers. It has useful sections on all the methods mentioned in the chapter.

Holly, M.L. (1989) *Writing to Grow: Keeping a Personal-professional Journal*. Oxford: Heinemann
A comprehensive book about the variety of writing styles that can be developed through the keeping of a personal-professional journal, ranging from therapeutic writing to logs of events.

Tripp, D. (1993) *Critical Incidents in Teaching: The Development of Professional Judgement*. London: Routledge.
If you are unfamiliar with critical incident analysis, this book will help you be more informed and feel confident in using this method in your research.

Wragg, E.C. (1999) *An Introduction to Classroom Observation* (2nd edn). London: Routledge.
Well written, comprehensive and extremely useful, this book tells you all you need to know about observation in the classroom. It has many useful pointers to how observation can enhance professional development processes and practices.

Dadds, M. and Hart, S. (2001) *Doing Practitioner Research Differently*. London: RoutledgeFalmer.
This book presents edited versions of practitioners' research reports and explores the motivations that caused the practitioners to break away from conventional approaches. Of particular interest are the chapters by Tish Crotty in which a fable is presented as a consideration of difficult issues, and by Liz Waterland where an imaginative reconstruction of several months in the life of a school is the focus of the research.

7 Critical Friendship, Critical Community and Collaboration

OVERVIEW

Similar to the approach used in Chapter 3, this chapter suggests ways in which practitioners in pairs or small groups can begin to explore the ways colleagues can be a useful resource in researching professional development and practice. There are sets of questions and activities to try which use critical friendship and critical communities to support your investigation.

The lonely researcher?

When you are carrying out research you can sometimes feel very isolated and there is often a sense of the 'loneliness of the long distance runner' in teachers' accounts of doing research (Campbell, 2002). Some of what has been advocated in previous chapters may appear to refer to individuals working by themselves, writing, reading and reflecting in lonely isolation. However, there is a need for a substantial recognition of the value of involving others, of collegial interaction, collaboration, peer scrutiny or review and of the role of others in providing challenges and different perspectives when researching into practice. Day (1999: 41) builds on the work of Ebutt (1985) in promoting the use of a critical friend/colleague to self-monitor practice in the classroom in an advanced model of teacher as inquirer working along a continuum spanning 'usual teaching mode to teacher researcher'. Day (1999: 144) states:

> Critical friendship is based upon practical partnerships entered into voluntarily, which presuppose a relationship between equals and are rooted in a common task of shared concern. The role of a critical friend is to provide support and challenge within a trusting relationship. It is different from the 'mentor' relationship in which one person (the mentor) holds a superior relationship by virtue of his/her experience, knowledge and skills. The critical

friend is recognised as having knowledge, experience and skills which are complementary.

While there is a notion of friendship in the roles of teacher as critical friend, collaborator and peer scrutineer, there is also a notion of challenge and confrontation for the purpose of development. Critical friendship and other relationships will involve disclosure and feedback. Talk is one of the main ways of conducting these critical friendships, peer scrutiny sessions and collaborations. In addition, being mindful of the developing use of new technologies, email, video conferencing, websites and chat rooms, for example, will all play a part in future exchanges and dialogues.

The following sites may be useful to visit, especially the CARN (Collaborative Action Research Network) and BERA sites:

- www.dfes.gov.uk/teachers/professional_development

- www.teach-tta.gov.uk

- www.ncsl.org.uk

- www.canteach.gov.uk

- www.carn.ac.uk

- www.bera.co.uk

The value of collegial discussion, collaboration, peer scrutiny and review cannot be overstated. Today's workplaces, whether in education or other related professional contexts, are far more collaborative than in the past. There is a tradition of 'coaching' and learning from 'master teachers' in the USA (Joyce and Showers, 1982), from which we could learn about collegial relations and developmental interactions. Similarly, Little (1982) wrote about the value of teachers engaging in 'concrete and precise' exchanges about teaching in order to improve teaching and schools. Eisner (1978: 622) wrote about the ideal situation:

> I would like one day to see schools in which teachers can function as professional colleagues, where part of their professional role was to visit the classrooms of their colleagues, and to observe and share with them in a supportive, informative and useful way what they have seen. Less professional

isolation and more professional communication might go a long way to help all teachers secure more distance and hence to better understand their own teaching.

In the last decade, it could be argued that practitioners engaged more regularly in discussions about the curriculum, planning, pupil achievement and progress. This is ostensibly one of the few acknowledged, visible benefits of the introduction of the National Curriculum in England and arguably one of the spin-offs of more overt teacher involvement, through mentoring, in the education, training and induction of new teachers. In recent years it has become much more common for there to be more than one adult in the classroom for most of the day. The appointment of a large number of teaching assistants, learning support assistants and learning mentors has contributed to existing arrangements with nursery nurses, care assistants and parents in classrooms. Due to inspection procedures and performance management practices, observation and giving feedback have become part of the accepted way of developing practice.

There is, however, a difference in what is meant in this context. What is referred to as critical friendship with reference to research methodology is a practitioner researcher who develops a critical community in order to interrogate and validate his or her research in a much more systematic way than the everyday occurrences outlined above. It requires a critical stance to be taken in order to provide rigour and depth of response. Becoming critical or acting as a critical friend, according to Macdonald (1986), gives teachers the power to determine their own agenda and to explore the role of theory in their teaching lives and may let them be in charge of the 'knowledge-creation process' instead of having the ideas of others imposed. Smyth (1991: 135) asserts that a critical pedagogy of supervision, used in the sense of appraisal of practice and 'supervising' or critically evaluating one's practice and the practice of others, is a powerful tool for reviewing and changing practice: 'Teachers working with other teachers to create a critical pedagogy of classroom practice through processes like clinical supervision can reveal the existence of a number of major impediments quite apart from the general issue of "Why would I want to do that, it sounds uncomfortable?"'

On occasions, being 'uncomfortable' results in some serious review and analysis of the 'taken for granted' practices we unquestionably employ on a daily basis. Smyth (1991: 113) advocates teachers engaging in four forms of action to develop a critical pedagogy of supervision:

1. Describe: what do I do?

2. Inform: what does this description mean?

3. Confront: how did I come to be like this?

4. Reconstruct: how might I do things differently?

Kennedy (1996: 22), a practitioner researcher, found:

> Using these four processes has liberated my ability to uncover much of my knowledge. I had at last found a structure that enabled me to see closely some of my values and beliefs and put them into words ... and peer scrutiny has provided me with some of the best insights into my own development and practice.

Exercise: starting a critical friendship

These four processes may provide a useful starting point for writing a piece to be shared with, or talked about with, a critical friend or group of critical friends. Choose a particular strategy that you would like to improve in your teaching and, on your own, systematically address the four questions above. When you have finished, spend some time with your critical friend discussing your responses.

How does critical friendship work?

A critical friend or 'significant other' can be anyone who has the ability to listen and to ask challenging questions. The meaning of critical in this context is worth brief reflection. The *Oxford Dictionary* and *Thesaurus* give the following definitions that may help to explain the role:

> expressing or involving an analysis of merits or faults of a literary or artistic work.

> a critical essay ... evaluative, analytical, interpretative, expository, explanatory.

Critical friendship provides both support and challenge to the practitioner researcher. Normally you would approach a colleague in your own school, a neighbouring one or a colleague with whom you have been attending course or network meetings. It is important to recognise that differing views may arise and that having a critical friend may not always be comfortable. You may have to agree to disagree. One major issue that has to be considered is that of confidentiality. Critical friends have to establish a trust and adhere to a professional code of practice that allows them to disclose professional and, at times, personal views that may be contrary to the prevailing norm in the institution in which they work. Indeed, they may be contrary to those of their 'other half'. A critical friend is a peer, a colleague and an equal. A group of critical friends could form a peer scrutiny group, looking at data, reading reports and generally engaging in collegial interaction.

A critical community is different from a group of critical friends. Normally a critical community would act as a 'validating group' that would 'comment fairly but critically on your research' (McNiff *et al.*, 1996). A critical community may include 'stakeholders' in the project and may also undertake a mentoring role, challenging and supporting through discussion, but also would be able to give advice and offer expertise in the area of research. A critical community may assess the research project and make valid the claims or findings of the research. (Further discussion and examples of a critical community are to be found later in the chapter.)

It is necessary for critical friends to devise ground rules for critical friendship duos, trios or larger groups, including issues to do with confidentiality, trust and other ethical concerns. The group should discuss and explore some of the questions below and agree a modus operandi. For a pair or small group to work well, each participant needs to make a commitment to the activity by allocating time for communication.

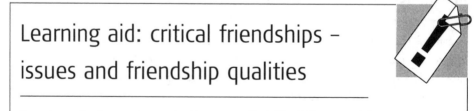

Learning aid: critical friendships – issues and friendship qualities

Some issues to discuss when embarking on a critical friendship are as follows:

◆ How do you establish trust between critical friends? What can be disclosed in a safe environment? How can it be ensured that these opinions will go no further than the group?

- How can agreement be reached on confidentiality issues amongst the members of the group?

- Who has responsibility for note taking or for feeding back points in the group? Will this rotate on a regular basis?

- How will the pair or group work? How often will there be meetings/interactions/communications?

- What roles and activities will the group engage in?

Some qualities to look out for in your critical friends are as follows:

- The ability to listen carefully.

- Interest and knowledge about the learning process.

- Empathy with adult learners.

- Ability to provide support in a variety of ways (e.g. experience in giving constructive feedback).

- Skill in asking probing and challenging questions.

- Ability to articulate ideas and beliefs, but also to be sensitive to others' opinions.

- Willingness to share expertise and knowledge.

The role of the critical friend is one that demands a great deal of patience, and listening more than talking. Egan's (1990) skilled helper model may be useful here.

Learning aid: the skilled helper model

Egan identified the skills of helping as follows:

◆ Exploring the concern by asking some open-ended questions, such as 'How do you feel about . . .? or 'Tell me about . . .?' or 'Can you explain . . .?' and avoiding expressions such as 'I think you should . . .' or 'I remember a similar thing once . . .'.

◆ Focusing on a specific aspect. It is essential to ensure that the choice of aspect is owned by the person being 'helped'.

◆ Considering new perspectives by asking 'In what ways might you . . .?' or 'How did this situation arise?' or 'Why did that happen?' or 'What do others think of . . .?'

◆ Setting realistic goals by being clear and specific about aims that are measurable and verifiable and in the control of your partner. Goals should be in keeping with the values of your partner and attainable in a reasonable time.

◆ Generating ways forward by focusing on action steps and asking 'How will you do . . .?' and generating a list of possible ideas for action.

◆ Planning precise action by producing an action plan. Agree first steps and anticipate support and pressures and plan ways of dealing with these. Agree a time line and a process of feedback and monitoring.

◆ Implementing the new approach or ideas by beginning a process of 'plan, do, review' similar to the steps in action research cycles, in order to monitor and reflect upon the implementation.

◆ Evaluating the new approach by formulating success criteria and a set of questions about the effectiveness of your approach or ideas.

The above structure can be more loosely followed in order to be more flexible and responsive to changing contexts, but as such could provide guidelines for developing a critical friendship. A crucial aspect of the pairings or groups is the forming of good collegial relationships, built upon trust and mutual professional regard.

Learning aid: questions a critical friend might ask

At the beginning of any research project the sorts of questions to be asked by a critical friend might include those that will help refine the focus of your research project, such as the following:

♦ What are the aims of the project? How do they fit with what you want to do? Can you clarify them further?

♦ What key words would describe your focus?

♦ Is the research concerned with evaluation of initiatives; personal experiences of teachers; pupils' learning; teaching strategies; or something else?

♦ What do you know about the topic already? How will you find out about previous research?

♦ How will you go about doing the research? What will you actually do?

♦ What do you hope to find out?

If you are involved in reviewing and researching your practice or professional needs and development and have undertaken some of the tasks in other chapters such as those in Chapter 3 about researching your professional identity, consider choosing a critical friend from among your colleagues or from within any network to which you belong. You could offer this person a piece of your reflective writing to read and discuss or you could ask him or her to interview you informally (see Chapter 6 for support and advice). It is always better to have something concrete to discuss as a starting point and to make an outline plan for the session.

Some examples of how a critical friendship might work are illustrated below as extracts from teachers' reports of their research of their professional development.

Illustration: teacher A (primary teacher) and diary writing

The use of a diary journal was an attractive method of collecting data on my teaching and I was able to use the data in my journal to help me analyse my current situation.

I found myself wondering whether or not I really was representing 'typical' incidents and episodes, or whether, indeed, my diary was building into a rather distorted image of my practice. This is why I found it particularly useful to submit my diary to the critical analyses of my fellow students on the course. Their responses not only directed me to consider the validity of what I had written, but, crucially, they highlighted for me some of the 'writing between the lines'. They focused my thinking by demonstrating to me that many, varied narratives were often motivated by the same underlying concerns, namely the tension between externally imposed demands and the conflict I perceived with my own professional sense of the best way for children to learn.

Teacher A used her critical friends to help her question the everyday occurrences that she was researching and helped herself develop a better view of what she was doing in her classroom and how this was informed by her beliefs and attitudes about 'good teaching and learning'.

Illustration: teacher B (special school teacher) and 'trusted colleagues' discussion group

I have benefited from being a member of an amazingly supportive group. They find time to listen and talk through issues with me and now I feel more able to support them. Discussion must occur with others if professional development is to occur but the others must be 'trusted colleagues' who have not only practical skills but also good social and communication skills. I feel privileged in that I could view any member of my group in this way. I also benefit from being a member of a multidisciplinary team who see issues from different perspectives. Motivation and the degree with which you are satisfied with your own work must play a factor in the reflection on practice and developing as a professional. I can't imagine ever feeling that I have finished learning or that I've got everything right. A group that asks challenging questions helps you to keep on learning.

The above demonstrates the reciprocity of the critical friendship role, where support and challenge allow the recipient of that support and challenge to engage in the same behaviour within the group.

Illustration: teacher C (science teacher educator) researching approaches to teaching

Discussions with critical friends have been interesting and occasionally controversial. Most of them share my view that science is not a body of facts but is a personal construct of our world. As such the methodology of science is the most important aspect of teaching it, because it is through this that we create our own constructs.

Discussion with G has led me to the writings of Popper, who said 'every recognition of a truth is preceded by an imaginative preconception of what the truth might be' (Popper, 1971: 56), thus advocating a creative approach to science teaching. This approach has been taken up by members of the group. S has done some work which he calls 'Tell me a story' in which he asks students to make up a story to describe what they see happening. Discussions with him have moved me into thinking of science in this more creative way. Another critical friend has discussed with me his desire to discover scientific truth. He reads of the theories of the great scientists and critically appraises them and tries to understand their scientific judgement and to fit these into his own framework. To be driven by the ideas of others is contrary to my philosophy but I cannot expect students to constantly re-invent the wheel for themselves, nor can I expect them to discover for themselves explanations that took years of thought and research. I am coming to the view that perhaps we should look upon science facts as scientific history. Collaboration and critical friendship has resulted in some agreement about approaches in teaching science.

Teacher C has engaged in an exploration and review of the theoretical knowledge and beliefs underpinning her practice with critical friends that did not always result in common understandings and agreement.

Illustration: teacher D (primary teacher) following an informal interview with a critical friend

Being interviewed about my beliefs and attitudes about teaching in such an honest way, and exposing all my inadequacies, brought back memories of school and failure and lack of support. My critical friend was exceptionally supportive and non-judgemental and wrote a very constructive response to the interview [see below]. He expressed similar experiences to mine relating to school days that have consequently shaped our beliefs. We talked about how important it was for teachers to know their pupils well and how experiences at school helped to generate a determination in oneself to know one's pupils well and to look for signs of dissatisfaction. He helped me to see the importance of developing a child-centred approach to teaching and learning. I had been fighting a system of traditional academic success and attainment throughout my own childhood experiences and in the schools where I had taught. I will research my teaching strategies in the light of these discussions and document the strategies I use to improve the learning in my classroom. I intend to read more about how to improve the teacher–pupil interaction and relationship in order to provide more opportunities for success.

Critical friend's response

It is clear to me that your own experiences of education have affected and shaped your beliefs. We began talking about your experiences of school and compared that with children's experiences today. These early comments introduced three main beliefs that you seemed to revisit throughout the interview: the need for teachers to know their pupils well; the crucial role that encouragement plays in improving performance; a belief in experiential learning.

Teacher D was helped to recognise and analyse her beliefs and attitudes to what was important in teaching and learning and to explore her own professional development areas for the future.

Other 'tried and tested' ways of using a critical friend are as:

◆ an observer of one of your lessons;

◆ a provider of post-observation feedback and critical dialogue;

◆ co-teacher and discussant; and

◆ co-planner and 'sounding board' for action.

Costa and Kallick (1993: 50) usefully describe the critical friend role as: 'a trusted person who asks provocative questions, provides data to be examined through another lens and offers critique of a person's work as a friend ... A friend is an advocate for the success of that work' and it is this person whom you can see as the common feature in the extracts quoted above.

Critical community

Having a group of critical friends, sometimes called a critical community, is another arrangement that allows you to take both the role of giver of support and challenge and receiver of support and challenge. Groups of practitioners and others in the local area (i.e. school(s), courses or networks and partnerships and, in some cases, national or international networks) can be established for the purpose of discussing and debating research projects and the resultant professional development.

A critical *community* is different from a critical *friendship* group as it would have more of a 'validation' type of role in a research project, although there is scope to vary the formality of any brief for the group from very informal and loosely structured to more formal and highly structured and organised depending on the nature of the research and the nature of the role of the critical community. It can often consist of those who are 'stakeholders' and 'experts' in the research area, and those who have an interest that may be 'academic' in nature.

Care should be taken to consider the role of each member of a critical community and to safeguard the researcher's interests and to prevent undue influence on the research project from those who may have a vested interest or 'stake' in the project. However small scale the research, it is important to ensure authenticity and validity within the research project and to consider whether what is being said or claimed is intelligible or meaningful; that what is claimed can be justified and that there is sincerity and merit in the communications (see Habermas (1972) for a full discussion of validity claims). There are several forms of validating procedures and a useful list can be found in McNiff *et al.* (1996), which covers a range of informal and formal styles across self-validation, peer validation, up-liner (management) validation, client validation, academic validation and general public validation. The choice of validation group is determined by the purpose of the research and the style, scale and scope of the research. In the context of this book, we are concerned with practitioner research in small-scale studies and a typical critical community might consist of the following.

Illustration: type A critical community

For a project looking at the use of group teaching strategies in the development of the use of ICT in the teaching of history:

◆ Fellow teacher researcher from network or course.

◆ Local authority adviser with an interest in the research area.

◆ Headteacher or interested governor of the school.

◆ Member of a national group or network who is an email contact.

Illustration: type B critical community

For a project looking at how one teacher uses questioning to improve his teaching in mental mathematics:

◆ Colleague from neighbouring school.

◆ Teaching assistant who works with the teacher in class.

◆ Head of maths department.

◆ DfES website chat-room contact.

Illustration: type C critical community

For a project looking at the development of the role of the headteacher in strategies for school improvement:

◆ Two local headteachers.

◆ Researcher from National College of School Leadership (NCSL) – email contact.

◆ Tutor in leadership and management from the local university.

◆ Headteacher of a well-known school which has pioneered strategies for school improvement through the use of Best Practice Research Scholarships.

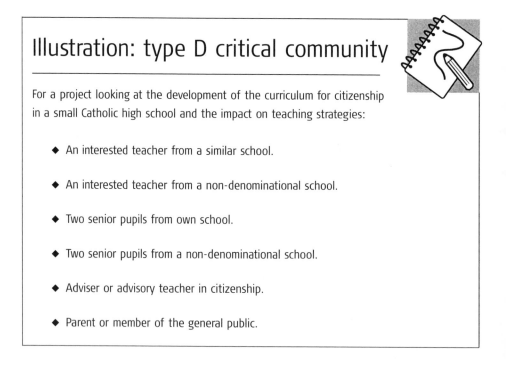

Illustration: type D critical community

For a project looking at the development of the curriculum for citizenship in a small Catholic high school and the impact on teaching strategies:

◆ An interested teacher from a similar school.

◆ An interested teacher from a non-denominational school.

◆ Two senior pupils from own school.

◆ Two senior pupils from a non-denominational school.

◆ Adviser or advisory teacher in citizenship.

◆ Parent or member of the general public.

The role taken by the members of a critical community can vary from that of discussant or 'sounding board' to adviser and expert. It is necessary to present your work publicly and to get views and opinions. Not everyone will agree with your research design and conduct or findings but it is important to document the views of others in a systematic way.

A critical community does not have to meet as a group, though face-to-face interaction yields good data and healthy dialogue. Communication can be by telephone or email or fax or in chat rooms and coffee bars on the Internet. All communications with the critical community should be documented and used as data in the research project. There are confidentiality and ethical issues to be considered by the critical community and it may be useful to have an agreed code of practice which establishes behaviour and responsibilities at the outset of the project. McNiff *et al.* (1996) have devised a useful set of briefing notes and, for more formally constituted groups on master's courses, criteria for making judgements about research projects. These could be amended to suit other contexts such as networks of practitioner researchers and small informal groups of practitioners in networked learning communities (NLCs) as currently being set up by the UK's DfES and National College of School Leadership (NCSL). Members of the critical community may have differing roles depending on their interest and expertise; one would not expect pupils to have the same role as an LEA adviser, for instance. Roles that can be undertaken by the critical community are listed below:

- Discussing ideas put forward by the researcher.

- Commenting on the draft reports (not editing).

- Trying out and commenting on materials.

- Providing knowledge and expertise in the research area and offering an 'informed' opinion.

- Providing a different perspective from that of the researcher.

- Asking 'difficult' questions and challenging assumptions.

- Supporting researchers in their development of ideas.

- Confirming the validity of the research.

- Commenting on the research design and project aims.

- Providing a critical perspective on the research.

It is the responsibility of the researcher to manage and organise the critical community, its role, function and identity. These aspects can vary greatly, depending on the individual specifications and requirements of research projects. For practitioner researchers, especially those concerned with investigating, reviewing and improving their professional development, it is essential that critical commentaries from colleagues in the field are documented and seen as part of the research process.

Collaboration, networking and critical appraisal are key aspects of researching professional development and therefore contribute greatly to the understanding of professional identity. Yet collaborative cultures are not 'cosy', as Hargreaves (1994: 195) states: 'in their more rigorous, robust (and somewhat rarer) forms, collaborative cultures can extend into joint work, mutual observation and focussed reflective inquiry in ways that extend practice critically, searching for better alternatives in the continuous search for improvement.' For a more personal approach, engaging in the types of writing and discussions advocated in Chapter 3 about exploring your professional identity may be a way into developing critical friendships and communities that support teacher learning and development. If you are engaged in, or contemplating, a research project or research activity, it would be useful to begin to identify a possible critical community that would be relevant to your concerns and to begin to think about the purpose, function and role that a critical community would play in your research. Map out a potential group and draft a brief for the group.

Mentors as support for research

This chapter has strongly promoted collaboration between teachers, practitioners and related individuals in critical friendship roles, peer groups and in critical communities in a variety of forms. It would be useful to explore, briefly, the role of mentor as different from the critical friendship and peer roles.

There may be some commonalities in the roles of critical friend, member of a critical community and mentor that could provide interesting comparisons and may illuminate practices, which could be adapted to enhance the various different roles. One aspect, which would appear to be common, is the reported benefits of collaborative work between experienced teachers and between teacher mentors and student or novice teachers. These reported benefits are in the resultant professional development experienced by all who engage in carefully structured and focused collegial interactions. Campbell and Kane (1998: 110) identify a strong relationship between mentoring and teachers' professional development in the areas of improved observational skills; developing new ideas and practices; and evaluating and appraising practice. Sachs (1999: 41) argues that: 'teacher research has the potential to act as a significant source of teacher and academic professional renewal and development because learning stands at the core of this renewal through the production and circulation of new knowledge about practice.'

Generally, a mentor has additional expertise to that of the mentee in the area in which he or she mentors. This is different from the 'buddy' type of approach being promoted in the critical friendship role and from the 'validating' role described for a critical community. As Edwards and Collinson (1996: 7) state in their discussion of mentoring in initial teacher education and training (ITET), mentoring: 'is used primarily to induct newcomers into the expectations and procedures that operate in a specific workplace . . . Frequently mentors have to take responsibility for teaching student teachers key aspects of their professional training.' Maynard and Furlong (1993) suggest that mentoring may also include 'co-inquiry', in tune with Russell and Munby's (1991) 'puzzles in practice' promoting collaborative examination of practice between mentor teachers and student teachers. There is a sense of the school or workplace as a 'learning community' where all participants are seen as learners. Stoll and Fink (1996: 156) linked peer mentoring with coaching and discussed the benefits in relation to school improvement strategies. Dallat *et al.* (2000) report on a project that meshed mentoring and teacher researcher approaches together in a way that enhanced mentoring and professional development, providing a 'bridge between scholarship and practice' (Fueyo and Koorland, 1997), and which allowed teachers, if they wished, to extend their initial research into a study for a higher degree which recognised and validated their professionally focused research projects.

The links between practice-centred initiatives and research activity are currently being firmed up and developed in England by the joint National College of School Leadership (NCSL) and DfES initiative 'Network Learning Communities' and other schemes promoting school-based research, where schools are being encouraged to bid for funding for projects aimed at developing the kinds of roles discussed in this chapter.

Looking ahead to the development of 'communities of practice' and learning communities, the practices developed in critical friendship models and collaborations offer a real opportunity for teachers and other practitioners to reclaim the agenda of appraisal, performance management and professional development. By using and publicising their professional development research projects, practitioners may help create the landscape of the future and establish practitioner research networks at local, national and international levels.

Further reading

Chapters 6 and 7 in McNiff, J., Lomax, P. and Whitehead, J. (1996) *You and your Action Research Project*. London: Routledge.
These two chapters, entitled 'Making claims to knowledge and validating them' and 'Making your research public', provide a good setting for the further exploration of critical friendships and critical communities. There are useful hints for getting work published in professionally focused locations.

Chapter 5 ('Teachers as collaborative and critical learners') in Smyth, J. (1991) *Teachers as Collaborative Learners*. Milton Keynes: Open University Press.
This chapter tackles how to bring about lasting, significant and meaningful change in schools by accepting the 'messiness' of development and the importance of ownership and collegiality and collaboration. Smyth's notion of 'clinical supervision' as a powerful tool in teacher development is explored and discussed.

The notion of coaching, first developed by Joyce and Showers (1982), may well be having a revival as teachers collaborate and develop ways of working together as critical friends. For a further exploration of coaching, see Joyce, B. and Showers, B. (1980) 'Improving in-service training: the messages of research', *Educational Leadership*, 37(5): 379–85.

Qualitative Data Analysis

OVERVIEW

In this chapter, we look at some of the features of qualitative data analysis and begin to unpick the strategies, skills and techniques you will need to develop in order to make sense of the data you have collected. We start by thinking about how the coding of qualitative data can be managed and discuss in detail the technique of open coding. We also consider, briefly, other techniques such as pen-portrait, metaphor and dilemma analysis that might be useful to you in developing an understanding of your data.

Introduction

Qualitative data analysis is a crucial part of the research process, yet typically it is clouded in 'mystique' and often not described in detail in reports of that research. This is in part because such analysis has characteristically been considered an interpretative art rather than a science, and hence a process that does not lend itself easily to simple articulation. Recent years, however, have seen a trend to more explicit discussion of qualitative analytical methods and this has been accompanied by an increase in the use, and sophistication, of computerised software packages such as QSR's NUD*IST and NVivo (www.scolari.co.uk/qsr) for the management and analysis of data. Generally speaking, investing in such software and spending the time to get to grips with it is probably not cost-effective for small-scale practitioner inquiry. An additional time/cost implication of using such packages is that the data would have to be held electronically in order to input it into the software program. Although we do not cover software analysis packages in this book, you will find increasing reference to them in educational literature and indeed they still require all the analytical skills and techniques outlined below – particularly open coding.

All qualitative data analysis is an 'interplay' between you, the researcher, and your data. The process is not just, or even centrally, objective, mechanistic and 'scientific' and it is important that you bring to it knowledge of life and literature, along with the necessary technical skills. So, for example, as we saw in Chapter 5, insights and theoretical frameworks from a wide variety of texts can be used as intellectual and practical resources for providing ideas, initial research questions and theories. This will include specialised or technical literature, such as research reports, sociological theories and methodological texts; but literary works, such as philosophical and historical writings, films and biographies, can also be a useful source of ideas. A cautionary note, however: although qualitative data analysis involves you using your knowledge and understanding of the world derived from experience or reading, it is important to be aware of any personal biases or preconceptions that may affect your data collection or analysis.

If that sounds a difficult enough task, it is also necessary for researchers to avoid 'going native'. That is, although they have to immerse themselves in situations and data and develop sensitivity and awareness of the subtle nuances of meaning, they should maintain a degree of 'objectivity' – an ability to remain at a certain distance from the research materials and characters and represent them fairly and impartially. You, as a practitioner researcher, have an even greater challenge in that you are a 'native'. This has tremendous advantages in that you have profound and extensive knowledge of the context you are researching but at the same time you need to develop the expertise to be able to look afresh, with a researcher's eyes, at everyday situations, habitual patterns of dialogue and interactions. In short, you need to develop the ability to reflect upon the familiar as unfamiliar.

The broader picture

Analysis is an integral part of the research process and so the methods employed should be consistent with the underpinning research tradition. In contextualist or interpretative traditions, for example, qualitative data are harvested mainly from interviews but they may also be forthcoming from open-response questions on survey questionnaires based in a more positivist tradition. The analysis of open responses to survey data has many features in common with the analysis of all qualitative data. One central difference between the two types of data is that it is possible, and often advantageous, to quantify qualitative survey data once they have been categorised and, in Chapter 9, we consider how this and other quantitative data from small-scale surveys can be managed, analysed and presented.

Before we look in detail at analytical techniques, however, it is worth reviewing, very briefly, the three important processes mentioned in Chapter 1: induction, deduction and verification. Social science, as well as natural science (so-called scientific) research, is subject to these processes and they are as important in the analysis of qualitative data as they are in the development of all scientific knowledge.

Induction leads the researcher from empirical observation to the development of a hypothesis. Such hypotheses are inevitably provisional and time and context dependent.

Deduction involves the researcher inferring the implications of current hypothesising and elaborating further upon the consequences. New hypotheses can then be developed and empirically tested against existing or additional data.

Inductive and deductive thinking are central to the process of constructing theory, as is the subsequent validation process. Although many would argue that much educational theory is descriptive, rather than explanatory, and thus not 'proper' theory.

Verification ascertains the integrity of hypotheses empirically – whether total or conditional or non-existent – and indeed the limits, if any, of their applicability.

The idealised model of inductive thinking leading to deductive thinking and so to validation (see Chapter 1, Figure 1.1) doesn't always materialise in reality, however, even in scientific research. Just as the relation between data and their understanding is problematic in social science research so too is it in scientific research. Rarely does scientific understanding and theory flow from unstructured observation. Most often in quantitative research data are collected with a hypothesis in mind, so observations are already geared towards those events that connect in some way to that hypothesis. Thomas Khun, famous for his reflections upon scientific method, observed that 'Numbers gathered without some knowledge of the regularity to be expected almost never speak for themselves. Almost certainly they remain just numbers' (1961: 45).

Equally well, theory often precedes scientists' ability to measure – the laws of planetary motion, for example, predicted the existence of a number of heavenly bodies many years before they were 'discovered' experimentally. Additionally, even when measurements are made they may not be understood; it was, for example, 25 years before experimental data which refuted the existence of 'ether', as a medium through which light was transmitted, were 'correctly' interpreted as such by the scientific community (Pawson, 1989).

Initially research in the social sciences adopted pseudo-scientific methodologies until the late 1960s when contextualist traditions (referred to in Chapter 1) began to take a hold and different analytical techniques were needed. Grounded theory was, and perhaps still remains, foremost in this field. It was devised by Barney Glaser and Anselm Strauss, whilst researching in the field of palliative care (their original book (1967) is quite a hard read and not to be recommended to the faint hearted). Grounded theory was a methodology in which theory was derived from data, systematically gathered and analysed; it offered a new way of studying social reality, which at the time was very novel and quite controversial. It was many years before it became accepted in the research world because it emphasised the building ('discovery') of theory rather than its testing ('verification'). Thus grounded theory was based on the 'logic of discovery' rather than the conventional 'logic of verification', which was more accepted in the still dominant positivist paradigm (see Chapter 1). The collaboration of Glaser and Strauss, fruitful for many years, ended acrimoniously, however, and both continued to write separately about grounded theory.

Grounded theory attempted to make data analysis a rigorous process and some would argue that in its earlier versions it attempted to replicate the perceived objectivity of the scientific method. In particular, it did not acknowledge the extent to which the interpretive framework held by the researcher/observer influenced the data collected and how they were perceived. So, for example, have you noticed that after becoming aware of something you have not previously observed you see it everywhere for a time. This is probably because you are sensitised to noticing it, which indicates that what you see is influenced by your personal theories about life. Language operates in the same way – the name of an object determines, or at least influences, what we think about it; which is of course the reason why marketing executives are so keen on re-branding products and organisations suffering from 'image problems'.

Nowadays many researchers claim to have used 'grounded theory' in their analysis, although in truth not many implement the complex procedures outlined by its designers to the full (a good example of an article that does use grounded theory to its full potential is Morrow and Smith (1995)). Although we do not have time to examine grounded theory methods in detail either, they do provide many rich and helpful insights into the analytical processes and in the section on open coding below we will attempt to indicate, in a much simplified fashion, some of the key features.

Techniques for analysing qualitative data

Analysis centrally involves the interpretation of data and it may be useful to begin by noting that the layers of complexity and construal of data are often threefold:

1. The actual events.

2. The accounts of those events given by observer/participants/researcher.

3. The subsequent interpretation of the accounts of the events by the researcher and others.

So it is important to remember that virtually all raw data are already a 'story' of an event – one person's account of that event from his or her very particular perspective. When you then add a further layer, that is, your interpretation of the data, it becomes a story of a story of an event, with the event itself (whatever that might be) gradually disappearing under layers of interpretation.

Having received that account, how do you prepare it for analysis? Ideally, the raw data would be in the form of a tape recording and along with this would be detailed 'field' notes recording contextual features relating to particular interviews. Details such as where and when the interview was conducted and particular characteristics and behaviours of the interviewee before, during and after the interview should figure in the material. If the interview is recorded in the form of handwritten notes then it is vital that as much as possible of the dialogue is written down verbatim. Tape recording an interview is preferable, not only because it is much easier for the interviewer, but also because it provides a far richer source of data for analysis; it captures speech inflections, pauses etc., which helps with interpretation. It is not necessary or even possible, however, to transcribe all of the interview. It can take anywhere between 5 and 10 hours to transcribe 1 hour of tape, depending on the clarity of the dialogue, background noise, the number of speakers, typing skills, etc., so it is important to be discriminating in the selection of excerpts to transcribe. Alternatively, analysis can be done straight from the tape.

Whatever course of action you decide upon it may be useful to listen to the tape and note down key points of the interview and the approximate position of these on the tape for future reference. An alternative would be to make brief notes relating to this during the interview itself, in chronological order so that the relevant extract is easy to locate. There is not the space here to go into detail about this data preparation phase but accounts such as that of Carole Cummings (1982) of her attempts to tape record the activities of her reception class one morning and transcribe the data would perhaps be interesting to peruse.

Analysis of qualitative data is complex because it involves two very different, and you may think contrary, skills. It necessitates you to be systematic and meticulous on the one hand and yet on the other creative (Strauss and Corbin, 1998). The process requires the ability to be able to:

◆ be open to the multiple meanings that the data offers;

◆ look at situations from different perspectives;

◆ think creatively in devising analytical/conceptual frameworks;

◆ make connections and apply relevant theoretical insights; and

◆ employ multimodal discourse (art, music, metaphor, etc.).

In this next section we will explore a number of techniques you may find useful to employ when approaching the analysis of textual data. The first, most basic and extensively employed analytical tool is coding, and we shall spend most time discussing this process which is at the heart of most data analysis. For many, or even most, research tasks coding and subsequently categorising data will be a sufficient analytic tool to identify relevant themes and understand what is happening in particular situations. We shall, however, very briefly consider other useful techniques that can be used along side coding: including metaphor and dilemma analysis and creating fictionalised pen-portraits.

CODING

Coding provides a mechanism for handling large quantities of raw data and how you chose to code these data will depend upon your particular project. The coding strategy may range on a spectrum from being, on the one hand, fixed before data collection. That is, data may be assigned to predetermined categories, as is often the case with closed questions on survey questionnaires. At the other end of the spectrum, codes may be entirely open and responsive to the data, that is, you may choose to use codes that emerge from the data. The conceptual categories, 'building blocks' of theory, once identified and developed, can later be integrated to form theory. We will focus in what follows on the kinds of skills that will enable you to open code data, and they are indeed generic analytical skills that will be useful to develop any reading of data. The likelihood is that the codes you will employ in the analysis of a limited-scale practitioner research project are somewhere between the two ends of the spectrum. That is, guided by your research questions, you will have some notion of the categories in which you are interested in collecting evidence and construct codes accordingly.

OPEN CODING

Open coding necessitates the researcher being, simultaneously, systematic and creative in his or her examination of the data. The process involves breaking data up into fragments, analysing their meaning and allocating codes to the concepts that are identified. The intention is not to come to a definitive answer but creatively to open up the possibilities.

This conceptualising is the first level of analysis and in this first instance it is helpful to give the phenomenon/event/action a name that is very closely related to it in some way, through, for example, imagery. These first codes should be a very close 'fit' to the data and can use actual words or phrases from the data. Glasser and Strauss (1967) recommend the use of actual words in the data and called these *in vivo* codes. Nearness to the data in selecting a code for the concept is vital as objects can, of course, be classified in multiple ways. A knife, for example, may be a culinary implement or a lethal weapon. It is important not to become too attached to these first codes, however, as they may become less significant as the entire data set is inspected.

Example: excerpt of interview data from a study of home-school links

Parent: If this Link project . . . is about [political agendas] asking parents to do the job that teachers are getting paid [demarcation of responsibility] to do I think that it is unfair.

Researcher: To whom?

Parent: Parent, child, but primarily the parent . . . we are **guilt tripped**. YOUR child is not **achieving** so YOU must do something about that [**responsibility**]. Most of us actually do want to do something but it has to be **fair** we want to take **responsibility** but they must take theirs [**demarcation of responsibility**] . . . if it is going to be a **partnership** we want a forum to speak [**political agenda**] . . . I'm fortunate I've had an education I don't feel intimidated by school and teachers, lots of parents do [**power relations**].

The example above shows an early stage of data coding from an action research and development project about home–school partnerships (McNamara *et al.*, 2000). The codes indicated in bold typeface include some codes that are *in vivo* codes (e.g. 'guilt tripped', 'partnership'); others are attached (e.g. 'political agendas'). It can be helpful, but is not always by any means necessary, to complete such detailed analysis of fragments of text, to look for ambiguities of meaning and articulations of politics/power/social dynamics, etc. However, the codes allocated to the fragment of data above give a good sense of what is happening. So, for example, two themes thread through the data: one is about intimidation, guilt, unfairness; the other is about partnership, responsibility and fairness. The data should be examined analytically and not just descriptively. Thus it is important to attend to not only *what* is said but also to *how* it is said, and what *effect* it has. What, for example, is the parent above telling us about herself, other parents, teachers and the dynamic between them in the sentence: 'I'm fortunate I've had an education I don't feel intimidated by school and teachers, lots of parents do'? Why does she feel she needs to say it?

If we consider this initial phase of open coding as a whole, characteristically:

◆ concepts are classified into categories related by common properties;

◆ categories are developed and subcategories defined; and

◆ analytical memos are written.

We will now look at these techniques in detail.

Creating categories

Creating categories is a process of grouping concepts that share common characteristics together under a more general category. Creating categories is important because it allows researchers to reduce the number of items they need to think about and move on from the stage where they can't 'see the wood for the trees'. Strauss and Corbin (1998) give the example of an observer reporting objects in the sky as birds, kites and planes. Recognising the common properties associated with all these phenomena in later analysis might usefully combine these conceptual codes into the category 'flight'. Categories are more powerful than single concepts in that they have analytic potential; that means that by comparing the relationship between individual concepts in a category the whole is more than the sum of the parts. For example, by associating birds flying with planes flying we can identify the various possibilities and constraints relating to aerodynamics and also where the analogy breaks down and why. There are drawbacks to this, though. For example, seeing the bird in terms of just one of its characteristics – 'flight' – is a shift that closes down certain avenues of inquiry in that the bird is now less likely to be seen as a part of the ecological system or the 'food chain'.

Developing categories

This involves identifying its properties or characteristics. In Strauss and Corbin's example above of the category 'flight', the properties of height, speed, distance, etc., are defined and the limits or dimensions of the properties recorded (e.g. height from very low to 35,000 ft). At this stage subcategories may be usefully identified within categories. These may be classified in relation to characteristics (type of flying object) or according to specific properties (speed of flight). In the development of categories it is important to find as many different cases of particular categories as possible and the data should be trawled to discover new examples. As far as possible the subcategories should be mutually exclusive – that is, they should not overlap – although of course it is possible that data extracts will be classified into more than one subcategory. Where possible the subcategories should also be exhaustive – that is, there should not be examples that do not belong in any subcategory. It may be possible that, for the sake of completeness, you might consider including a subcategory for which no instances/examples can be found in the data in order to draw attention to that very fact.

In the home–school partnership project mention earlier (McNamara *et al.*, 2000), for example, the authors identified the subcategories shown in the example below in relation to the category 'parents supporting their children's learning'.

Example: subcategories of 'parents supporting their children's learning'

encouragement, 'he gets 110% encouragement in everything he does';

praise, 'I told him it was great';

surveillance, 'he is not allowed not to do his homework. I check his book a lot and his journal';

criticism, 'I sent him back many a time and told him that's rubbish';

teaching, 'I don't tell them the answer I help them to figure it out for themselves';

resource support (material) 'I bought extra books'

(and strategic) 'I read a bar of chocolate helps, the sugar boosts'; and,

bribery, 'If he goes to school he gets £1.50 spends in the evening for going' (McNamara *et al.*, 2000: 478).

Writing analytical memos is a vital form of aide-memoire in the analysis process. They are akin to field notes in the data collection process and should record recoding activity, relationships between categories, the development of theories, evaluative or reflective thinking. Analytic memos, like field notes in a research diary, should always be dated and contain references to any related documents. The example below illustrates analytical notes made for a meeting early in the analysis phase of the home–school links project described above. It was an example of an analytical framework derived from a 'market driven' model. The idea was rejected because it was relatively limited in its applicability to the data, as its explanatory power in relation to the entire data set was not extensive enough.

Example: analytical notes

3.01.99

The internal market of performance indicators was complex for parents to interpret and navigate. They found it 'very hard to understand'. It required an understanding of the exchange rate/reference system and knowledge of the value of the child within it:

'5 credit = 1 letter home then silver, gold and prize'.

Parents habitually experienced problems of calibration concerning:

measurement ('I wasn't actually sure how it was measured');

consistency ('I beg your pardon I have just been told the opposite');

frequency of calibration ('once a year [for reports] is not good enough');

meaning ('it went up to 6.3 which Dominic was very pleased about. 6.3 what?').

Sometimes they rejected information on the basis that it made them anxious about how much their child was valued: 'I do and I don't . . . information makes you more anxious about how well your child is performing.'

Once the initial phases of the open coding and category development are complete, you should begin the validation processes. It is important to examine the data actively for 'negative cases' to ensure that you have not been overtly biased in your selection of examples. Once you are convinced your analysis has been fair it is time to establish your 'findings': the statements you can make in relation to your data analysis. A final stage, and one that is probably not appropriate or necessary for most limited-scale practitioner research projects, is developing a theory from the analytical framework: finding a way of conceptualising the data as a whole that integrates the categories you have identified. We will now look at each of these elements of the process in a little more detail:

◆ Theoretical sampling.

◆ Negative case analysis.

♦ Interrogating data to ascertain findings.

♦ Developing theory.

Theoretical sampling

This is the stage in the analysis process when the theory drives the data collection rather than vice versa, where the data can be scanned quickly and compared to the categories. Have you identified all examples of categories and subcategories? With your categories in mind, sieve through the data and ask questions about additional categories or subcategories or boundaries between categories. Have you categorised all the data relating to the initial questions? You may decide to go out and find data that have not so far emerged naturally to answer one of your initial research questions. Or perhaps the data that have emerged in particular categories may lead you to pose further research questions that need to be answered.

Through this process of sampling and constant comparison of categories by examining their boundaries and looking for similarities, differences, explanatory usefulness, etc., categories may be combined or regrouped and new categories discovered or developed. When no further categories appear to be emerging the theoretical framework is said to be saturated (Strauss and Corbin, 1998). It is also vital during this phase of analysis always to be on the lookout for counter-examples or *negative cases*, which appear to contradict the themes that are emerging. So, for example, in the home–school data above we looked for examples of occasions when parents felt it inappropriate to support their children's learning.

Interrogating data

Interrogating data will be the final stage for most limited-scale practice-focused research projects. This can be carried out once you have settled with confidence on your complete analytical framework, which may have emerged predominantly in response to the initial research questions you posed. You are now in a position to ask yourself what statements or claims you can make in respect of it. So, for example, if you were inquiring into parents supporting their children's learning one of your initial research questions might have been to discover the extent of parents' involvement in homework activity. One or more of your analytical categories would most certainly have related directly to this. It could be that your prime interests in this area related to the differences in parental support of boys and girls, or the variation in their support of children at different phases of their schooling. If this was the case these over-riding interests would have guided the configuration of your categories.

The types of claims you may wish to make about the data include descriptive claims such as the approximate number of parents who help their children with homework and the average amount of time spent each night by these parents. It is important to qualify such descriptive statements, not necessarily with percentages, but most certainly with adjectives such as 'nearly all', 'most', 'many', 'a few'. You might also want to break down the reporting of these data in relation to key variables such as gender and age. Alternatively, you may wish to make explanatory claims about the reasons that parents claimed they did, or did not, become involved in their children's homework. Again, this may be with respect to age and/or gender. You may want to make claims about children's or parents' attitudes towards parents helping their children with homework. Finally, you may wish to make evaluative claims about the effect, or effectiveness, of parents supporting their children with homework from the perspective of the parents, the child or perhaps the school.

Developing theory

This is the final stage of this process and involves identifying the main theme of the data. Generally, it will be one core category or categories that integrates most of the other categories and has the greatest potential to explain or describe what is happening. So for example, in the home–school project described above, which had as its central focus parents supporting their children at home, having rejected a theory based upon an internal market (and a couple of other ones along the way) we settled for the twin core categories of 'mobilisation' and 'demobilisation'. These military metaphors seemed to have considerable explanatory power for the data set as a whole and a matrix was developed involving parent, child, teacher and school. Categories of mobilisations and demobilisations were identified between each of these participants and theoretical sampling was undertaken to explore further categories or properties of categories.

So, for example, we identified that school mobilised parents by enlisting their help as supporters, decision-makers, supervisors and teachers. On the other hand, and sometimes simultaneously, schools alienated their children's parents in a number of ways, some of which are illustrated in the following example.

Example: the ways in which schools alienated their children's parents

academically, 'the whole system and language around the system is very difficult, they all alienate us';

physically, 'the thing that upsets me the most was that I couldn't get up the stairs';

culturally, 'forcing house of the middle classes . . . hidden curriculum . . . preparing kids for company life';

religiously, 'whether mums aren't appreciative of me because of me not being Catholic';

psychologically, 'you need a lot of confidence to contact a school';

technologically, 'there were computers everywhere and it was dead hi-tech';

socially, 'it's all like the boundary/demarcation . . . bringing your social life into school;

ideologically, 'if this link project is about asking parents to do the job that teachers are getting paid to do I think it is unfair'.

We will continue this chapter by considering very briefly three other types of analysis that you may find useful to employ alongside the basic open coding technique.

METAPHOR ANALYSIS

Metaphor analysis is 'good as a way into understanding how participants conceptualise and feel about their activities and roles' (Somekh, 1995: 65). Metaphors depict one thing in terms of another and, because of this, they often exaggerate or parody the way people feel about what they do and they draw attention to features of particular significance or pathos. Somekh (1995: 65) suggests that the researcher should:

1. search for and highlight every metaphor in the transcript/text/notes;

2. identify one overarching or significant metaphor;

3. use this metaphor as an analytic tool to gain further leverage on the data. How far does all the data 'fit' the metaphor? Where/how does it not fit?

In the case of the home–school link project we used the military metaphor 'mobilise' as a core category (or meta-metaphor) but examples of other metaphors used in the data of the project are italicised in the excerpts shown in the example below.

Example: metaphors identified in home–school project data

Parent of school:

I think there is a lot of pressure for parents, I think parents are *hunted* as extra help to make sure that their child is *pushed.* I do all sorts of things for the children because at the *end of the day* you feel as if your children should be at a *higher level* than they are.

Parent of child:
She is a *leech* a *bloodsucker* . . . she takes advantage. James is the *postman* but the letters always get lost!

Parent of teacher:
A latter day *Wackford Squeers* . . . *machiavellian,* he ruled by fear.

In another research project, focusing upon the training of primary teachers, a number of metaphors were identified with varying degrees of explanatory usefulness for different purposes and occasions. The metaphor of 'game', for example, featured very prominently in a number of trainee accounts such as the excerpt shown in the example below.

Example: metaphors used by trainee teachers

Well I know I know in school, I know definitely part of the **game** for me, and I had to learn the hard way, was you know, if you are gonna **get through** this you better be submissive. Sometimes you might need to have to go to someone for some advice when you didn't need the advice. You knew the answer but maybe you needed to go and ask that person, to make that person feel good about themselves. So in school I realised that the **game**, **the game** in school, when you go in school is really to get on get on the **best side** you can with the teacher. Don't **rock the boat**, because from the minute you **rock the boat**, that's it you don't stand a chance at all of **getting anywhere**. So that's the **game** there.

Finding this theme in the data together with much reference to 'ordeals' and 'symbolic acts' and 'ritualised behaviours', we subsequently drew on a theoretical perspective from anthropology and worked with a notion of initial teacher training as a rite of passage. You will find this referred to briefly in Chapter 10.

DILEMMA ANALYSIS

Another useful way to get into the data is through looking at tensions or dilemmas. Somekh (1995: 66) describes dilemma analysis as: 'good for understanding the values and tensions which frustrate or fascinate the participants. Very useful if the patterns are later used to focus discussion between concerned participants who have differential power/status in the same institution or social setting.'

She advises analysts to:

a. Search for and highlight any passages in the transcripts/text/notes which show hesitancy, puzzlement, uncertainty, a sense of difficulty or stress in the participant.

b. List each of these 'dilemmas' on a sheet of paper expressed in the form:
One the one hand . . .
On the other hand . . .

c. If you can manage it, the two statements should be balanced in being as far as possible neutral statements of each opposing point of view/belief/value (i.e. even if you can see the participant leans more heavily to one point of view than the other).

d. If possible, carry out dilemma analysis of a number of interviews with participants who have differing perspectives and differential power/status in the situation.

e. Put dilemmas into a single list, without indicating from whom each originated, and use this list as a discussion document with all the participants.

In the project relating to the trainee teachers a number of dilemmas were identified, such as the ones shown in the example below.

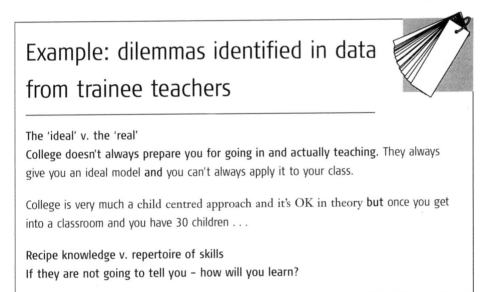

Example: dilemmas identified in data from trainee teachers

The 'ideal' v. the 'real'
College doesn't always prepare you for going in and actually teaching. They always give you an ideal model and you can't always apply it to your class.

College is very much a child centred approach and it's OK in theory but once you get into a classroom and you have 30 children . . .

Recipe knowledge v. repertoire of skills
If they are not going to tell you – how will you learn?

Metaphor and dilemma analysis can be useful to give an extended understanding of the complexities presented in the data and they are described in more detail in Altrichter *et al.* (1993) and summarised in Somekh (1995) in her helpful and very brief review of analytic techniques. Another analytical technique presented by these authors is pattern analysis. Valuable as a way of identifying 'routinised or ritualistic behaviour', they suggest identifying patterns occurring in the data and discussing the meaning they may have with participants and how other people might regard them.

PEN-PORTRAIT ANALYSIS

Biography, pen-portraits and fictional critical writing, mentioned briefly in Chapter 6, are useful devises to employ if you want to illustrate and disseminate participants' perceptions, experiences and feelings in a lively, authentic, meaningful and accessible way. Traditionally, research and evaluation projects report an analysis of issues, activities and contexts that characteristically fragment and decontextualise individual histories to a large degree. Biographical techniques, such as developing pen-portraits, remedy this significant potential defect by presenting data in the form of a vignette, or thumbnail sketch. The vignette would be fairly brief (one to three pages perhaps) and most probably targeted at a particular aspect of the participant's professional life or activities rather than attempting to convey a wide-ranging life history. Aside from serving a reporting function in themselves, pen-portraits can be used as professional development materials in order to highlight particular issues. An alternative to this straightforward biographical account is to create vignettes from amalgams of individual characteristics across the entire data set, thus developing 'fictional' pen-portraits. We will now consider the analytical steps that would lead towards the development of fictionalised pen-portraits and, centrally, these rest upon open coding, as outlined in the main part of this chapter.

A biographical pen-portrait will of course be drawn from just one interview. Fictionalised pen-portraits, on the other hand, necessitate a data set of perhaps about 15 interviews. The first three steps set out below are common to both sorts of pen-portraits but the remaining five relate to fictional accounts only.

Learning aid: the steps involved in creating a pen-portrait

1. The first step involves you in open coding the interview transcripts in the manner described above to identify issues, characteristics, key factors, critical incidents, etc. – depending on the theme of your research and nature of your interview schedule.

2. Highlight in the transcript quotations, metaphors, dilemmas, patterns of behaviour, etc., that exemplify key issues arising from the analysis.

3. Weave them together in a vignette (see Chapter 10 for an example) which depicts the individual history of the participant in respect to the matter being considered using these key verbatim quotations, characteristic and issues, etc.

4. To create fictional pen-portraits you will need to compile lists of issues, characteristic, activities, experiences, dilemmas, etc.

5. Highlight in the transcript quotations, metaphors, etc., that exemplify key issues arising from the analysis as above.

6. Analyse the distribution of these issues across variables that are relevant to your interviewees (teacher/pupil) such as key stage, age, experience, ability.

7. Create a list of 'ideal types' of pupil/teacher. In the example below is a list of some of the teacher types that two of the authors constructed from data collected in the case-study phase of a baseline survey of teachers' perceptions of CPD.

8. Finally 'fill out' these ideal types with actual experiences, quotations, perceptions, attitudes that are relevant to the character you are depicting from across the entire data set.

Example: ideal teacher types
identified in a baseline survey of CPD

Anna
Bright-eyed and bushy-tailed, a 23-year-old newly qualified primary teacher just finishing her first year. Has been superbly mentored, has extensive professional development portfolio and a clear plan for her career progression in the next five years.

Brian
A cynic, aged 48, who came into teaching from a career in industry and has been teaching for 18 years in 3 different secondary schools. Has a great deal of enthusiasm still for his subject, English, but that's about all! Doesn't have much truck with CPD, finds INSET days a waste of time, but thoroughly enjoys taking his pupils into London to 'do' the shows.

Andy

Ambitious, committed and 35 years old. He has worked in the same medium-sized special school, for children aged 4–19 with moderate learning difficulties, since joining the profession 7 years ago. Member of Senior Management Team, Special Needs Co-ordinator and responsibility for Personal Social and Health Education. The school has an extremely well organised professional development programme that is based on the appraisal/ performance management system co-ordinated by the head.

Linda

29 years old, been teaching for 5 years in the same primary school. Did a BEd at the local university. Getting somewhat jaded but recently had a 'road to Damascus' experience on CPD course with thinking skills guru and is now totally enthused and sees it to have had real effect upon her classroom practice.

We will look further at aspects of the relative value of these two approaches to pen-portrait analysis when we consider what the completed products might look like, and how they might be used. We will do this when we begin to look at writing up and reporting of research.

The analysis of qualitative data is undoubtedly the most challenging research skill to master. It will require time, sensitivity to nuances of meaning and a degree of aptitude to accomplish well. Furthermore, facility at data analysis alone is not sufficient; as a researcher you will need not only to be able to interpret data but also to convert them into information, articulate that information and communicate it to interested parties. You will find advice and support in relation to this aspect of the research process in Chapter 10.

Alongside interviews, small-scale questionnaire surveys are perhaps the most popular and useful form of data collection for practitioner researchers. Question-naires are commonly used to generate both quantitative and qualitative data and in the next chapter we will consider in some detail the management and analysis of the quantitative data.

Further reading

Altrichter, H., Posh, P. and Somekh, B. (1993) *Teachers Investigate their Work*. London: Routledge.

This is an immensely useful guide into action research methods for first-time researchers in education and the social sciences. In particular it has a very useful chapter on data analysis.

Strauss, A. and Corbin, J. (1998) *The Basics of Qualitative Research: Techniques and Procedures for Developing Grounded Theory*. Thousand Oaks, CA: Sage.

This is the main grounded theory text cited in this chapter. The first edition of this book was published in 1980 but, sadly, Strauss died just before this second edition was published. It is probably one of the best overviews if you want to get into grounded theory seriously and most certainly a lot more accessible than the original Glaser, B. and Strauss, A. (1967) *The Discovery of Grounded Theory*. Chicago, IL: Aldine.

9 Quantitative Data Management, Analysis and Presentation of Questionnaire Surveys

---

OVERVIEW

In this chapter we consider how to manage and analyse quantitative data generated from questionnaire surveys, but the techniques described are equally useful for quantitative data from sources such as structured observation. Building upon the discussion in Chapter 6 we identify key types of survey questions and consider how the data generated by them might be coded and recorded. We offer one way of calculating some simple descriptive statistics using Microsoft Excel spreadsheet and, finally, we describe how Excel's Chart Wizard can produce simple graphs, bar charts and pie charts to portray the data in an accessible and attractive format.

Introduction

Questionnaires are a very versatile data-gathering method; they are cheap, easy to administer, whether it be to three people or 300, and can be used to gather a great variety of data of both a qualitative and quantitative nature. Data collection is, of course, not the only function of a questionnaire: they can serve to raise awareness of particular issues and make respondents feel valued and important elements of the decision-making process. Questionnaires, as well as gathering information, can also be instrumental in educating – opening respondents' eyes to particular ways of looking. So, for example, the authors were part of a team that conducted a baseline survey of teachers' perceptions of continuing professional development. In the construction of the questionnaire we thought carefully about the way the balance of questions relating to traditional (conferences, courses, etc.) and non-traditional (peer coaching/observation, reading, research, etc.) CPD was informing respondents' perceptions whilst they were completing it.

Chapter 6 alerted you to the kinds of things you need to think about when constructing your questionnaire and outlined some basic design features. It made it clear that there was a balance to be had between response rate, on the one hand, and length, complexity, density and coverage on the other. Every question you put into a questionnaire is at the expense of another, so it is important to prioritise the information you really need. Psychologically, for a small-scale questionnaire, two sides of A4 is really the maximum and it should be attractive (colour and Clip Art if you can manage it), structured into sections if it lends itself to partitioning, and include instructions relating to completing and returning that are easy to read and understand. Include, if possible, an addressd envelope or a fax-back number to facilitate ease of response.

A questionnaire can be used to generate a number of different types of data. You may want to gather descriptive data, which would include information about preferences, personal histories, events, etc.: the 'what', 'how often', 'where', 'when' type of question. Alternatively, you may want an insight into respondents' attitudes and perceptions – 'how do they feel?', 'what do they think?' etc. Or you may want explanations – to know, for example, the reasons why prospective pupils and their parents choose your school. Finally, you may want evaluative information – how effective or valuable did the parents find your open evening?

We will now consider five question response types that are generally considered the mainstay of questionnaire design, namely:

1. category

2. quantity/information

3. rating scale

4. ranking

5. open response.

A questionnaire may contain just one type of question response or could, and most usually does, have a mixture. The advantages of using a mixture of response-type questions – in terms of gathering a range of data, maintaining a reasonable level of interest and avoiding patterned responses – must be weighed against the disadvantage of requiring respondents to understand and respond appropriately to different instructions. We will shortly think about each type of question and consider how you would go about coding, recording, analysing and reporting the data gathered. Data analysis, as noted in Chapter 6, is an important factor to consider when you are designing a questionnaire. You need a clear view of how you would code and analyse each question before you commit yourself to it; there is no point in asking a question if you haven't got the capacity to process the data generated by it.

Data management and coding

CATEGORY RESPONSE

The age and gender questions in the example below are category response questions. In compiling such questions you must ensure that the categories you choose are mutually exclusive (i.e. there is no overlap between categories and only one response is legitimate for any one respondent) and exhaustive (i.e. coverage is total and every respondent can find a relevant category). If there is any doubt regarding the exhaustiveness of the possibilities on offer, a category labelled 'other' should be added.

The analysis of closed response questions, like that of the qualitative data we saw in the last chapter, begins with a coding process. The difference is that in the case of closed response questions coding is a very mechanistic process. So, for example, in questions 1 and 2, in the example below, the respondent was a male and aged between 30 and 39.

Example: category response questions

1. Age group	20–29	
	30–39	✓
	40–49	
	50–59	
	60–65	
2. Sex	Male	✓
	Female	

Supposing 39 people responded to these particular questions; the information could then be collated in a simple tally chart, as shown in the example below.

Example: tally chart to record category response data

	Category	Tally	Frequency
1. Age group	20–29	1111 11	7
	30–39	1111 1111	10
	40–49	1111 1111 11	12
	50–59	1111	5
	60–65	1111	5
2. Sex	Male	1111 1111 1111 1111	20
	Female	1111 1111 1111 1111	19

The disadvantage of recording data in tally charts is that potentially valuable information, relating to the responses of individuals across a number of questions, is lost. So, for example, analysis of the pattern of responses of men/women or younger/older respondents as distinct groups would not be possible.

An alternative recording system involves allocating a code to each category response using a simple coding system. A coding strip attached to the grid in the example below (to the right of the grid) shows how the responses to those questions might be coded using a simple system in which 30–39 would be coded '2' and male '1', etc.

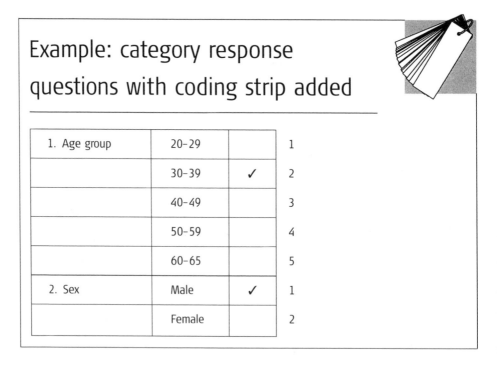

Example: category response questions with coding strip added

1. Age group	20–29		1
	30–39	✓	2
	40–49		3
	50–59		4
	60–65		5
2. Sex	Male	✓	1
	Female		2

Instead of using a tally chart such as the one shown above, the coded data would then be entered into a grid. A small part of one such grid is shown below. In this example each row represents a different questionnaire response (T1, T2, T3) and each column represents a different question number (1, 2, 3, etc.). It will be helpful when you are setting up the grid to attach a simple descriptor to each question number. A grid recording system such as this will allow you to retain all the details of the information supplied on individual questionnaires.

Example: grid to show recording of coding data

	1 age	2 sex	3 school	4 KS	5 role
T1	2	1	2	3	2
T2	3	1	1	4	4
T3	1	2	5	3	3

You can enter this information on a simple grid drawn using the 'Table' facility in Microsoft Word or, alternatively, and more powerfully, you can use a spreadsheet such as Microsoft Excel. Excel is an excellent software package in which to record and manage data – not only because, as a spreadsheet, it is a ready-made grid and has the facility to work out frequencies but also because it can very easily produce a variety of attractive graphs for the subsequent presentation of those data.

QUANTITY OR INFORMATION RESPONSE

The 'length of teaching experience/time at present school' and 'main post of responsibility' questions shown in the example below require an open response but of a very restricted nature: a quantity in the case of questions 3 and 4, and information in question 5. Questions 3 and 4 can, if helpful, be retrospectively grouped into time categories and coded in a similar way to questions 1 and 2 above. Question 5 can again be coded retrospectively giving posts of responsibility that occur most frequently an individual code and grouping and coding minority responses together into an 'other' category.

Example: quantity or information response questions

3. Length of teaching experience	_____ years
4. Length of time in present school	_____ years
5. Main post of responsibility in present school	_____

LIST RESPONSE

Question 5 above specifically asks for the 'main' post of responsibility in the school, thus forcing a singular response. It may be that the respondent actually had multiple responsibilities and this would be particularly useful to know. In this case the question could be rephrased as a list question, such as question 6 shown below, where it may be appropriate to tick more than one response.

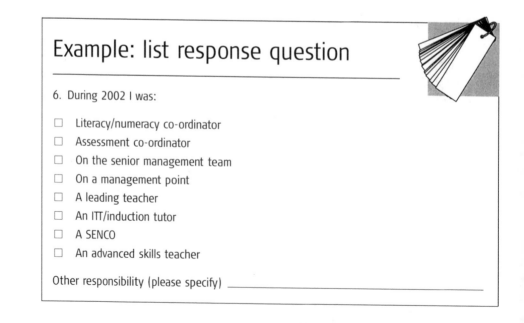

Example: list response question

6. During 2002 I was:

☐ Literacy/numeracy co-ordinator
☐ Assessment co-ordinator
☐ On the senior management team
☐ On a management point
☐ A leading teacher
☐ An ITT/induction tutor
☐ A SENCO
☐ An advanced skills teacher

Other responsibility (please specify) _____

Since respondents to question 6 may tick more than one box, each of these responses will require an individual response column in your grid. The responses in the 'other' category can be coded retrospectively if sufficient numbers or important themes emerge. The coding of such a question is shown below. Here the codes 0 and 1 are used to indicate nil and positive responses to the question from the six respondents. Respondent 6, for example, was an advanced skills teacher on a management point who was also an induction and ITT tutor and a governor of the school (retrospectively coded as 3 in the 'other' category).

Example: coding a list response question on a spreadsheet

Question 6
Post of responsibility during 2001

	Lit/num	Assess	SMT	Man pt	Lead T	ITT/IND	SENCO	AST	Other
T1	1	0	0	1	0	0	0	1	0
T2	0	0	0	0	0	0	0	0	1
T3	1	0	0	1	0	1	0	0	0
T4	0	1	0	1	1	0	0	0	0
T5	0	0	1	1	0	0	1	0	0
T6	0	0	0	1	0	1	0	1	3

RATING SCALE RESPONSE

Questions which ask respondents to rate their feelings or attitudes against a prepared scale are the mainstay of questionnaire design. The correct name for such a scale is a Likert scale. One decision to take here is whether to have an odd (usually three or five) or even (usually four) point Likert scale. This will generally depend upon whether you think it valuable, for your purposes, force respondents to come down on one or other side of a positive/negative 'divide' or to give them the option of a more neutral 'don't know/not sure/no change' central position. A second decision you must make is whether to attach descriptors to categories, such as the ones shown in question 7 below.

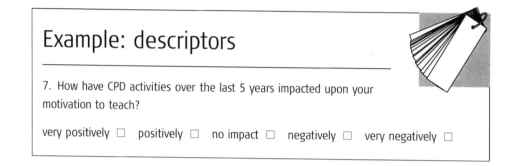

Example: descriptors

7. How have CPD activities over the last 5 years impacted upon your motivation to teach?

very positively ☐   positively ☐   no impact ☐   negatively ☐   very negatively ☐

This can be very expensive in terms of space on the questionnaire but, where you can combine a number of such questions with the same descriptors in a grid-type format (such as in question 9 below), it becomes more feasible. Question 8 illustrates an alternative format in which only the extreme ends of the scales have descriptors.

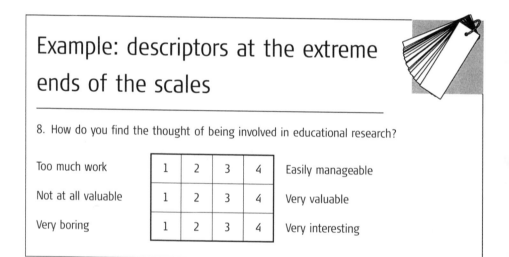

Example: descriptors at the extreme ends of the scales

8. How do you find the thought of being involved in educational research?

Too much work	1	2	3	4	Easily manageable
Not at all valuable	1	2	3	4	Very valuable
Very boring	1	2	3	4	Very interesting

Example: rating scale question

9. How much information about teaching do you gain from . . .

	None	Little	Some	A lot
Professional journals	1	2	3	4
OFSTED/HMI	1	2	3	4
DfES	1	2	3	4
LEA	1	2	3	4
Books	1	2	3	4
Press and media items	1	2	3	4
Professional unions	1	2	3	4
Universities	1	2	3	4
Colleagues	1	2	3	4
Conferences	1	2	3	4
Other . . . (please specify)	1	2	3	4

The coding strategy for these questions is self-evident and often (as is the example above) the code is included in the question cells and is actually circled by the respondent. Some researchers believe that, so as not to confuse respondents where you have a number of such questions in a questionnaire, you should maintain the same coding strategy – that is, a 1 for a 'negative' response and the highest score for a 'positive' response (or vice versa). An alternative argument is that varying the coding strategy keeps the respondent alert and avoids 'patterned' responses.

The example below shows how question 8 and part of question 9 would be entered in a grid or spreadsheet. You will notice that the columns relating to question 9 are shaded. The reason for this is that it is helpful to put down markers (shading or an alternative format) on particular questions in order to help you keep a check that you are entering the data in the correct column where you have a long string of numbers.

Example: coding of rating scale response question on a spreadsheet

Question 8			Question 9				
The thought of being involved in research			Information about teaching gained from				
Manageable	Valuable	Interesting	Journals	HMI/Ofsted	DfES	LEA	Books
1	3	3	1	2	2	3	4
2	2	2	2	2	2	2	3
3	4	4	4	3	3	3	3
3	4	4	4	3	3	3	2
2	4	4	4	3	3	3	3
3	4	4	3	2	3	3	2
1	2	2	3	3	3	2	2

RANKING RESPONSE

These questions require respondents to rank a number of options in a particular order. Question 10 is an example of such a question but do beware when you include rating scale and ranking questions in the same questionnaire that you make the distinction between them very clear. Once set into a particular pattern (e.g. rating), respondents often need a real jolt to alert them to the fact that the question requires a different kind of response. Ranking response questions again force a particular coding strategy; that is, of course, 1, 2, . . . 6 in this example.

Example: ranking response

10. Below are some immediate responses from teachers when asked what they thought of as CPD activities. Please RANK them in order from 6 (your most likely immediate response) down to 1 (your least likely immediate response).

Courses/conferences/workshops	[ ]
Watching and talking with colleagues	[ ]
School INSET days	[ ]
Personal research and reading about education	[ ]
Online learning	[ ]
Training	[ ]

OPEN RESPONSE

Open response questions are a must for questionnaire surveys if only as a 'catch-all' at the end to give respondents the opportunity to reveal any ideas/comments/suggestions they have been harbouring and not had the opportunity to articulate. But they are also valuable to explore more freely perceptions and attitudes. Questions such as 'What image does educational research conjure up for you?' can generate so many rich data that they make the extra effort required in the recording and analysis worth while.

This particular question was used in a questionnaire eliciting teachers' experiences and perceptions of being involved in research (reported more fully in McNamara, 2002). Indeed, a number of the examples in this chapter have been taken from that particular questionnaire. In the case of this specific question, the responses were collated and themes identified. Typing the responses as a list is very time-consuming but does make the analysis process much easier. We chose to partition the emerging themes into the six broad categories, which each had a number of sub categories, as outlined below.

Illustration: what image does educational research conjure up for you?

1. Researchers as:

   ◆ academic

   ◆ utopian

   ◆ out of touch with real classrooms.

2. Research process as technical:

   ◆ statistical data

   ◆ scientific jargon controlling variables and testing hypotheses

   ◆ questionnaires, graphs, surveys, observations, asking questions.

3. Research process as teacher/school-based:

   ◆ action research as instrument of change

   ◆ assessment of current practice and justification for good practice

   ◆ looking in detail at teaching/learning.

4. Impact on education:

   ◆ no evidence of impact

   ◆ implications for action not clear

   ◆ teachers on the ground left to implement.

5. Feelings towards research:

   ◆ exciting and interesting

   ◆ worthwhile

   ◆ hard work.

6. Politicised context:

   ◆ misinterpretation of findings

   ◆ manipulation of findings

   ◆ ignoring implications that didn't find favour.

Having identified such themes it is important to complete your analysis by calculating the relative weighting of each theme in the data: was the image of research as 'technical', for example, more prevalent than research as 'teacher/school-based'? The degree of accuracy with which you do this will be a matter of choice and dependent on factors such as audience and style of reporting. For most purposes descriptors such as 'many', 'most', 'few', etc., will be quite sufficient. At the other extreme you could allocate each theme a number and code the open response questions in the grid with the rest of the data in order to use the statistical and graphing facilities of the spreadsheet.

Data analysis

CALCULATING FREQUENCIES

Having discussed at length different types of questions typically used on a questionnaire, and how to code and record data generated from each, it now remains to explore how to compute some simple descriptive statistics in relation to those data. A small portion of data is shown in the example below and you should be able to follow the instructions given in this section if you copy these data into an Excel spreadsheet. The data show the response of ten parents from St John's primary school to questions 1–5 of a questionnaire. The column (A–F) and row (1–12) identifiers (shaded in the example) are part of the pre-existing structure in the Microsoft Excel spreadsheet. The identification given to each questionnaire as it was entered is in column A (J5, J6, etc.). The question numbers are written into row 1. Question 1, for example, asked 'what is your relationship to the child?' and four categories of response were offered: mother, father, carer and other. Question 2 asked the sex of the child. So, for example, the 2 in cell C9 tells us the child referred to in response J11 was a girl and the 1 in cell E7 tells us that the parent in response J9 was not at all satisfied with the preschool provision her child attended.

The maximum number of codes used in any one question in this questionnaire was five. In order to work out the frequencies of the responses to each question the numbers of responses categorised as 1, 2, 3, 4, 5 need to be totalled (i.e. the frequency of response in each category calculated). Nil responses should be left blank. Importantly, if you wish to code and total nil responses then enter them with a zero but the response codes will now, of course, be 0, 1, 2, 3, 4, 5.

Example: a section of a spreadsheet showing the coding of data from a questionnaire

	A	B	C	D	E	F
1		1 relation	2 sex	3 preschool	4 satisfied	5
2						
3	J5	1	2	3	3	5
4	J6	1	1	2	4	2
5	J7	1	2	3	3	2
6	J8	1	2	3	2	3
7	J9	1	2	1	1	3
8	J10	1	2	2	4	5
9	J11	1	2	3	3	3
10	J12	1	1	4	3	3
11	J13	1	2	1	2	2
12	J14	1	2	1	4	3

We are now going to consider how these codes can be totalled to discover the *frequency* of each response to a question. Some questions might only have two or three possible responses and thus codes; question 2 is one such example. Indeed, every question could be dealt with separately and the formula used to find the frequencies customised but, in order to take advantage of the power of Excel to repeat operations, we will describe how to total each question as if there were the same number of responses (in this case five). If there were fewer than five possible responses, the frequencies of the codes that were not used will not be a problem as they will appear as zeros. If there are additional codes over and above five because, for example, you decided retrospectively to partition the 'other' category of one question and used extra codes (over five), the numbers of these will be collected together in an extra 'bin' as we will see below. A most valuable feature of the Excel spreadsheet is that if you change any data number after the frequencies have been calculated the frequencies will change automatically.

First copy the small section of data shown in the example above into a Microsoft Excel spreadsheet and follow the procedure for working out frequencies as follows.

The first step is to input the codes you are going to total:

1. Leave a row below the bottom of the data entered in rows 1–12 and, in column B rows 14–18, key in the numbers 1, 2, 3, 4, 5 in cells B14–B18.

2. Highlight the cells in the block B14–B18 and along to F14–F18.

3. From the Edit drop-down menu, select Fill and from the Fill submenu, select Fill right.

All the cells you highlighted should now be filled with the numbers 1, 2, 3, 4, 5 (as shown in the example below).

The second step is to prepare the array in which your frequencies will be dumped:

1. Highlight cells B20–B25. You need to highlight six cells in this example: five cells to collect the frequencies of the responses coded 1–5 and one to dump any higher values you may have entered (always highlight one more cell than you have codes).

2. With this array highlighted, put your cursor in the formula line (at the top of the screen directly beneath the toolbars). Enter the formula: =FREQUENCY(B3:B12,B14:B18). This will tell the program to total the numbers in rows B3–B12 with respect to the numbers in rows B14–B18 and to dump the frequencies in the highlighted cells B20–B25.

3. When you have entered the formula correctly, press Control + Shift + Enter. Totals (the frequencies for each code) should appear in cells B20–B25, in this case (10 0 0 0 0 0). Curly brackets will also appear automatically around the formula.

The final step is to copy this formula across the rest of the data:

1. Highlight cells in the block B20–B25 and across to F20–F25.

2. Go to the Edit menu and select Fill from the drop-down menu. Select Fill right from the submenu.

The frequencies of the different responses to questions 2–5 should now appear in the cells highlighted, as is shown in the example below.

Example: a section of a spreadsheet showing frequencies of responses

	A	B	C	D	E	F
		1 relation	2 sex	3 preschool	4 satisfied	5
1						
2						
3	J5	1	2	3	3	5
4	J6	1	1	2	4	2
5	J7	1	2	3	3	2
6	J8	1	2	3	2	3
7	J9	1	2	1	1	3
8	J10	1	2	2	4	5
9	J11	1	2	3	3	3
10	J12	1	1	4	3	3
11	J13	1	2	1	2	2
12	J14	1	2	1	4	3
13						
14		1	1	1	1	1
15		2	2	2	2	2
16		3	3	3	3	3
17		4	4	4	4	4
18		5	5	5	5	5
19						
20		10	2	3	1	0
21		0	8	2	2	3
22		0	0	4	4	5
23		0	0	1	3	0
24		0	0	0	0	2
25		0	0	0	0	0

Further help on the topic of 'Array formulas and how to enter them' can be found on the Help package in Microsoft Excel. You will find there are alternative ways in which to calculate these totals and one is through the COUNT function which can also be found on the Excel Help package.

MEAN SCORE

Before we go on to consider how to present this information visually it is perhaps worth mentioning briefly a measure you might want to consider calculating for rating scale questions and this is a mean score or average of the responses. For many questions, such as numbers 1 (relationship of respondent to the child) and 2 (sex of the child) there is no meaning to be assigned to an average response. For rating scale questions such as the ones shown in the example above, however, you can calculate an average score that is both meaningful in itself and also allows you to compare the responses to different questions, or indeed the responses of different groups to the same question. It is, of course, easier to compare across questions if you have used the same number of points on all the rating scales (e.g. either all four- or all five-point Likert scales).

The calculation of mean scores is very simple. Let us take as an example question 4, in which respondents were asked to rate their satisfaction with their child's preschool experiences against a four-point scale. To calculate the mean score, all you have to do is divide the total of the scores (in this case $3+4+3+2+1+4+3+3+2+4=29$) by the number of respondents, in this case 10, giving an average of 2.9.

This can again be worked out quickly on Excel using the AVERAGE function. Working on the same data recorded above, highlight cell B26 and enter =AVERAGE(B3:B12) in the formula line at the top of the screen. Then press 'enter' this will take the numbers in cells B3–B12, work out the arithmetic mean and put the answer in cell B26. Using the Edit, Fill, Fill Right procedure, the rest of the averages for questions 2–5 can be computed giving the answers below (most of which you will recall are not actually meaningful):

	B	C	D	E	F
26	1	1.8	2.3	2.9	3.1

Note: A combination of the SUM and COUNT functions =SUM(B3:B12)/COUNT(B3:B12) will do the same.

If you are using a tally chart rather than a spreadsheet you can also calculate the mean score quickly and simply. You already have the scores grouped and the frequencies (total numbers) in each group so you can use that information: 1 person responded 1, 2 responded 2, 4 responded 3, and 3 responded 4. In order to find the sum of the scores everyone gave to question 5, simply multiply the frequencies (the number of people in each group) by the respective scores and add them together. To find the mean score, divide that sum of scores by the number of people who responded to the question (that is, the sum of the frequencies). The calculation is set out in the example below.

Example: calculation of mean score

Score	Frequency	Score × Frequency
1	1	1
2	2	4
3	4	12
4	3	12
Total	10 people	29 score

The mean or average score for this rating scale question is then calculated by dividing the sum of the scores (the total of the score × frequency column) by the number of people who responded (the total of the frequency column), which gives 29/10 or 2.9.

Data presentation

The final step in the research process is of course the reporting stage, and Excel is very effective at generating graphs and charts to represent data. We will take you through one such operation but encourage you to explore the many different types that are available. You should by now have a copy of the table we have been working on in an Excel spreadsheet. We will use as an example the data in column D relating to question 3: 'What preschool provision did your child attend?' The frequencies of the responses to question 4 are in cells D20–D23. Highlight these cells and click on the Chart Wizard (the bar chart icon) on the toolbar (or, alternatively, on the Insert drop-down menu). The wizard is very user-friendly and instructs you through each of its four steps. In the first step you are offered the possibility of 15 or so graphs and charts of 'standard types' and another 20 or so 'custom types' (the actual charts offered will vary slightly with the version of Excel you are using). You are also offered the possibility of seeing a sample of what the graph would look like for the data you have highlighted. Click on some of graph types to explore the possibilities. As you will see, most of the standard and custom types plot the raw scores – that is, the number who responded to question 3 with a 5, 4, 3, etc. If instead you would prefer a diagram that gives you percentage responses for each category, go for a pie chart. In the 'standard types' window the pie option has six different types and there are two further options in the 'custom types' window – a black and white pie and an expanding blue pie chart. We will now draw a black and white pie chart from our data but all the pie charts basically follow the same four steps.

You should still have cells D20–D23 highlighted (the responses to question 3). In the Chart Wizard go to the 'custom types' window and take the option of the black and white pie; you will see a model of what it will look like. Select the Next option, which relates to the data source. The Data Range and Data in Columns buttons should be highlighted as default options. Select the Next option again and you will be offered the possibilities of entering 'titles', 'legends' and 'data labels'. Select 'title' and enter the title 'What preschool provision did your child attend?' on the title bar. You will see the title appear on the model. Move to the 'legend' window and you will be given the option to choose whether or not to include a legend and if so where to place it. Tick the legend box and you will see it appear on the model. Deselect the legend box on this occasion as we don't want to include a legend and instead move on to the 'data label' window and highlight the 'show data label and percent' button. Select Next and you will be presented with options relating to the location of the new chart. You can choose to put it as an object in either the same sheet that the data are currently located in or a new sheet (chart 1). Choose the Same Sheet option and select finish and the chart will appear immediately in the middle of the page; you can now move it and/or resize it as you please in the same way that you would any object.

The final stage of the process is to make the pie chart more meaningful for, although it already has a title, the data labels with each percentage are numbers. In order to replace the data labels with pertinent words, single right click over data label 1 and all the labels will be selected. You will be given the option of formatting the data labels. Select this option and you will be given the choice of various formatting features such as font size. Deselect format at this point, and left click on label 1 instead, a text box will appear around it. Place your cursor in the text box and replace the label '1' with the more meaningful identifier such as 'day nursery' (take care not to delete the percentage). Repeat the procedure replacing labels 2, 3 and 4 with 'playgroup', 'child minder' and 'children's centre' respectively. If need be, return to the reformat option to change the font size or style. In addition to changing the format features of the pie chart, you will also be able to change other features. As well as resizing the frame (that is, the chart area), you can also resize the plot area – the pie chart itself. If you single left click just below the pie you will see highlighted the plot area, which directly inscribes the pie chart. By manipulating this you can resize the pie as a whole or individual sectors of it.

Your pie chart should now resemble that shown below. Having prepared the pie chart you can copy it into a Word document to use it in a report or print it on to an overhead transparency for presentation at a conference or in-school meeting. It is important to note that if you leave the pie chart on the Excel data sheet any changes you make to the data will automatically alter the frequencies and the sizes of the sectors on the relevant pie charts. However, depending on which pie chart you choose, the changes do not always alter the written percentage in the data label. In the case of the 'blue pie' on the 'custom types' window the percentages are written on the sectors of the pie itself in the plot area and they will change automatically as the size of the sectors change when the data are altered. If the percentages in the data labels do not change automatically they will have to be altered manually using the procedure outlined above for changing data labels. Once the pie chart is pasted into a Word document you will have even less flexibility to change it, certainly with the earlier versions of Excel. The best solution is simply to keep copies of the charts in Excel, make any changes there and paste revised versions into the Word document. It is worth noting that Word files with Excel charts in can grow to quite some size.

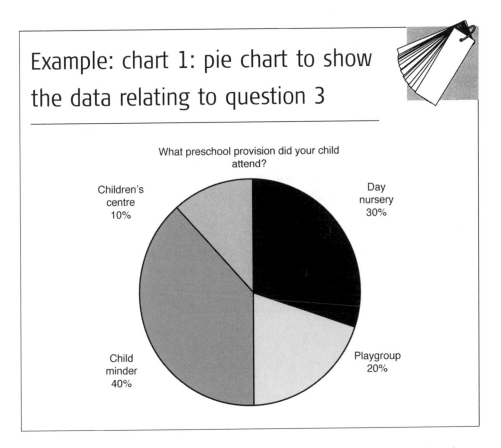

Example: chart 1: pie chart to show the data relating to question 3

What preschool provision did your child attend?

Children's centre 10%

Day nursery 30%

Child minder 40%

Playgroup 20%

There are many other options to explore for drawing graphs using Excel and you will find that you can quickly become a confident user of the charting function. Accessible information that looks very professional can be produced quickly and to great effect from raw data. Should you wish to produce illustrative charts from existing data that have already been collated you can simply enter them as a column in Excel and go through the procedure for drawing charts outlined above.

In this chapter we have introduced you to some possible ways of recording, managing and analysing quantitative data in order to prepare simple descriptive statistics. In particular, we have introduced you to some of the features of spreadsheets such as Excel. If you require any more complex statistical tests to be carried out on the data a package such as SPSS, a statistical package for the social sciences, would be required but it is very complex and you would need professional training to use it. We have also described how you can use Excel's excellent graphing features to represent your data in an attractive and accessible format in written reports and persuasively in presentations. We take up the theme of the oral presentation of data further in Chapter 11 and talk about written reports in Chapter 10.

Further reading

Munn, P. and Driver, E. (1995) *Using Questionnaires in Small Scale Research.* Edinburgh: Scottish Council for Educational Research.
This is a useful sourcebook which gives a practical guide to using questionnaires in small-scale research.

Bell, J. (1999) *Doing your Research Project.* Buckingham: Open University Press.
This immensely popular research methods reader has been mentioned before but particularly note that it does contain useful chapters on 'Designing and administering questionnaires' and 'Interpretation and presentation of evidence'.

10 Writing up, Reporting and Publishing your Research

OVERVIEW

In this chapter we look at the writing up or the reporting of the research process. It is a vitally important stage yet it is one that many very busy practitioners, driven by the desire to improve their practice, will find it difficult to prioritise. We consider the types of research writing that you may become involved in and the factors that will influence your decision, such as intended purpose, audience, genre, etc. We focus particularly upon three different forms that your writing up may take: reporting, writing for publication and the construction pen-portrait materials that could be used as catalysts for professional development activities as well as serving a reporting function. We discuss the process of writing itself and the different ways the literature you have read and used in your research can be incorporated, and we alert you to some of the issues you need to think about with regard to finding an appropriate publishing outlet and tell you what the process might involve.

Writing up: genres, purposes and audiences

Stenhouse's (1980) seminal definition of research as 'systematic inquiry made public' takes as implicit and fundamental that your ultimate ambition will be to disseminate the findings of your research in the public arena. This may involve an oral presentation at a conference/meeting or a written (used in the widest possible sense) account in the public domain. You may well have discovered for yourself by now that the reporting of research is extremely varied in nature, style, quality, length, accessibility and relevance to practice. At worst it can be impenetrable, a consequence not always of the author's preferred style, but of current funding-related pressures on academics in the UK to publish in prestige journals, where high competition can lead to esoteric intellectualism.

Bassey (1995) suggests there are three types of research writing:

1. *Academic mode*: to be found in academic books, refereed journals and conference papers. The audience is largely other academics.

2. *Professional mode*: to be found in professional journals, magazines and newspapers. Its purpose is to 'add to practical knowledge' and its audience is mainly practising professionals, teachers and others engaged in the educational service.

3. *Pedagogic mode*: to be found in research assignments, dissertations and theses. Its purpose is to 'demonstrate to a tutor, and possibly an external examiner, that the student is learning to conduct systematic, critical and self-critical enquiry'.

The likelihood is that your writing may combine elements of at least two of these three genres. It is in fact very difficult to be prescriptive about the form your writing might take because, of course, this will vary considerably depending upon its:

◆ *aim* – e.g. to describe a situation, to inform action, to report to parents, etc.

◆ *purpose* – e.g. accountability, accreditation, pleasure, impart knowledge, etc.

◆ *audience* – e.g. principally practitioners and their immediate professional contacts (such as teachers in their school, other teachers, parents, pupils or other educational stakeholders, academics, etc.).

◆ *form* – e.g. entirely textual or multimodal, containing perhaps video or audio recordings, links to websites; entirely web based, etc.

◆ *length, style* and *genre* etc.

◆ *eventual destination*:

   ◇ whether you hope to publish and, if so, whether in a newspaper, professional or academic journal, website, electronic journal, etc.;

   ◇ whether you intend to present at a conference and, if so, who will be the audience and what technological facilities will be available.

It is important that you are clear in your mind about these issues and if you have been commissioned/awarded a grant to do the research by someone else (e.g. your school, a funding body), it is important that you also consult them regarding their understanding of these issues (preferably before you accept the commission). So, for example, do they want you just to conduct a baseline survey or come up with some recommendations? In the case of grants awarded for research, the form and, hopefully, the audience and purpose, of the final report will have been thought through and most probably defined in the tender document or the contract.

If you are a free agent it is not necessary, and perhaps not even helpful, to decide on the exact format of your report before you begin writing up. We make this point because it is unrealistic to consider matters such as your aspirations to publish your report before you have even identified your findings; but it is very important that you do not leave all your reporting/writing until this stage. There is nothing so intimidating than an imminent deadline and a blank page – even seasoned writers can find this quite threatening.

There are certainly sections of the writing up that can and should be put together before the final stages of the analysis are complete. You may feel you have plenty to do at this stage and not see writing as your priority, but not only will this strategy preclude writing blocks potentially occurring at a later stage, it will also help you think though methodological issues and may perhaps expose weaknesses. It is often at the stage when you set things down on paper, or rehearse a presentation, that you begin to firm up your line on exactly what you are doing and ask yourself challenging, and yet sometimes very obvious, questions about the methodology.

It is vitally important for the wellbeing of practitioner research, especially in education, that teachers themselves, or teachers in collaboration with HEI colleagues, should not only become involved in doing research but also be seen to be involved in its dissemination. Teachers have traditionally been reluctant to become involved in this final phase of the research process, and Somekh (1993: 176–9) outlines a number of reasons why it is especially important for them to make their knowledge public:

◆ Public reporting prevents teacher knowledge from being forgotten.

◆ The process of reporting teachers' knowledge increases the quality of reflection on practice.

◆ Through reporting research, teachers clarify their own position and bring influence to bear on educational policy by means of rational augment.

◆ By reporting their research knowledge, teachers meet the requirements of professional accountability.

◆ By making their research knowledge public, teachers can play a more active role in teacher professional development and initial teacher education.

◆ By reporting their research knowledge, teachers reinforce their professional self-confidence.

◆ By reporting their research knowledge, teachers improve the reputation of the profession.

Legal and ethical considerations

It would perhaps be useful at this point to remind you briefly of issues relating to legal and ethical considerations, specifically as they relate to confidentiality, ownership and management of data, copyright and intellectual rights. These matters can be tricky to negotiate and there is clearly potential for concerns relating to them arising in a close-knit community such as a school. The situation is complex and always subject to local individual agreements but, generally, you will always have 'intellectual rights' over your ideas and writing (unless the research is carried out for your employer and your contract of employment specifically waives your right to this). If you publish in a journal or book, however, the copyright may reside with the publisher. This means that, technically, if you wish to reproduce the article elsewhere, you will have to ask their permission and they may, although it is unlikely, ask for a small fee. If you were commissioned or awarded a grant to do the research you may need to consult your contract – it could be that the funder retains ownership of the data and copyright over the report. The funder may well also want to vet other publications.

Complications in relation to copyright are extremely unlikely in small-scale practitioner research but one thing you will need to be aware of is the new Data Protection Act 1998 which came into effect in the UK in 2000. The new Act has extended the scope of the previous Act in a number of ways. The regulations now apply to non-computerised records – including microfilm, videotape and electronic data, as well as computerised records. Individuals must be informed of the purposes for which their personal data will be processed and to whom they may be disclosed. Processing here means obtaining, recording or holding the information or data or carrying out any operations on it, including alteration or disclosure. The processing of sensitive personal data, including those relating to racial origin, religion, political opinions, physical/mental health, etc., has been made subject to even tighter control. Finally, the rights of data subjects have been extended, including their right of access to the data and to have them erased or rectified, or to prevent them being processed in certain circumstances. If you are in any doubt about the data you hold and the way in which you intend to process them it is very important that you read the regulations in detail (http://www.dataprotection.gov.uk) and perhaps take advice on the matter. Research in the UK that involves access to any part of the National Health Service in particular is now subject to very strict ethical protocols and guidelines to which you have to adhere (see the examples at http://www.mmu.ac.uk/rdu/).

Be particularly vigilant if your research includes questionnaire and interview-based research involving confidential or sensitive issues, or contact with subjects who might be regarded as dependent, such as children or persons with some form of disablement. Additionally, if your data include any image-based records of clients, especially children, this can be a very sensitive matter to negotiate. You will obviously have requested permission to collect data before you embarked upon your enterprise. You may not, however, have been specific at that point about exactly what the data collection involved and what was to be done with them – or indeed your plans and intentions may well have changed during the course of the project. Go back to check exactly what parents/teachers/pupils have given their consent to. Were you very clear when you sought permission what you were to going to do with the data (e.g. restricted use of data within school, publication, publication of video images, publication as still images, online images, etc.)? Remember that when it comes to sanctioning such a request clearly the appropriate line manager (e.g. headteacher) bears the ultimate responsibility.

Writing for a report

It may be that the format of your research report is prescribed in detail and leaves little to the imagination. If this is not the case then perhaps, as a starting position for teachers, we could suggest the following possible format for a standard four-page summary report which could be distributed around your school, other schools in the LEA or posted on a website. You will find an example of a completed report using a similar style of proforma in the resources for research.

TITLE

If possible make it short, snappy and lively with perhaps a more explicit subtitle (e.g. 'Fun and phonics: teaching reading to poor readers in Year 5').

AIMS OF THE PROJECT

Include here the central aims of your research (which may include pedagogic as well as research aspirations). They may change slightly over the course of your project so don't necessarily feel obliged to stick to the wording of the ones you identified initially. If the aims have changed considerably and your work was externally funded you may perhaps need to consider consulting the funder before making the decision to change tack. In most cases all that will be necessary will be an admission that your original plans changed and an explanation of why. This could be included in the 'reflections on the research' section or at some other point.

FINDINGS

Include six or eight bullet points here. For example:

- ◆ Girls responded positively to a female role model.

- ◆ Parents reported pupils showed increased confidence and self-esteem. Staff involved claimed to be more confident in teaching science.

- ◆ There was no evidence of raised numeracy levels as a result of the booster programme. (*Note*: Don't feel you must only report the positives.)

This first section would be akin to an executive summary in a traditional report and the remaining sections would fill in the detail regarding background and evidence base.

BACKGROUND

Give a brief synopsis here of the background to the research inquiry. Describe the educational situation in your department/class/year group. You will probably need to include relevant details of the school context. Include information on the issue of concern, the research question(s) and what led you to ask these particular questions.

LITERATURE REVIEW

Outline what understandings (if any) you gleaned from an initial review of the literature. Summarise other research projects that have been carried out in the area. What were the findings? How did the review inform your understanding of the situation? What are the practical, educational and political implications surrounding the area in which you are researching?

THE PROJECT

Describe the planned developmental process (if there was one). Give details of the intervention programme. Who was involved? When and where did it take place?

The research process

Describe the data collection process. How did you decide upon the sample – which pupils and/or classes to track? Did you have any baseline data? What methods did you use – interviews/questionnaires/video/observation? What issues arose for you as a teacher doing research? Were there any conflicts/ethical issues between your teacher and researcher selves?

RESULTS

Include in this section the themes that emerged from the research, which will relate to the findings/results outlined on page 1. A short paragraph focused upon each will be sufficient. Make the results as interesting, meaningful and accessible as possible. Don't just stick to prose. Where possible include easy-to-interpret tables of data and charts (if appropriate). Likewise, include vivid and detailed descriptions of individual case-study data (if that is appropriate for your study). You may have interviewed some children or got them to complete diaries, so include some short quotations – they make compelling reading.

REFLECTION/EVALUATION ON THE RESEARCH

Did you carry out your research as planned or were there any unanticipated hitches? Were there or may there in the future be any unanticipated outcomes? One of the themes should most certainly be a reflection upon your/your colleagues' increase in knowledge, skills and understanding of curriculum and research matters and professional development generally.

IMPLICATIONS FOR TEACHERS/TEACHING

These might just expand on the findings and might include: suggestions or reflections on what you would do differently next time; how you could further improve your intervention programme; or the costs and benefits of getting involved in teacher research.

IDEAS FOR FURTHER INVESTIGATION

Things you didn't get round to; what other related avenues need investigating.

FURTHER READING AND BIBLIOGRAPHY

It can be useful to separate these two. Aside from a conventional bibliography teachers find a 'further reading' section helpful. This should not be extensive, just three or four curriculum/research-focused articles that you found particularly interesting or informative, with perhaps a brief sentence about each, similar to the style we have adopted in this book.

Writing for publication

It may be that your aim is to publish an account of your research, in which case a narrative form might be more appropriate than the report style outlined above. Generally speaking, your options are threefold: academic journals, professional journals or the popular press. The latter would include publishing in a newspaper or commercial journal such as *The Times Education Supplement* or *Child/Junior Education*. Sometimes such outlets pay for contributions and commission work, but don't give up the day job as the remuneration will not be substantial.

If your aspiration is to publish in professional or academic journals then clearly the 'higher' your ambition – in terms of publishing in prestige journals – the more competitive you will find it. Generally speaking, any articles you submit to academic journals will be subject to peer review and be more competitive to access than professional journals that tend to be managed by editorial teams alone. Having said that, a number of academic educational journals like to publish the work of teachers, and may, like *Educational Action Research*, offer editorial support/advice to teachers in preparing their articles for publication.

Identifying an appropriate journal to target is not always easy; it may be that there are some specific to your area of interest, in which case searching the library journals catalogue will help you to identify them. It is important, having located them, to spend time flicking through recent issues on the library shelves to become familiar with the house style, more of which below. If no outlets come to light immediately you will have to do some research. This is particularly important in the case of general education journals because they are a lot more difficult to typify; the territory may be largely unfamiliar and you may not even recognise the names of the contributors. Browse the shelves of the library, ask the journals librarian for help, as they may be able to direct you, and look at the journals that are coming up most frequently in the reading you are doing. Whilst browsing the library shelves for possible outlets, try to get a sense of the house style of the journals; there may well be some explicit information regarding what kind of articles the journal is willing to consider and also the intended audience. What is most difficult is fixing the standard of the journal. In order to attempt to do this, look at the quality of the writing, the length of the articles and the eminence of the contributors. If they are all professors from top-flight universities perhaps you should not target it for your first attempt at publication.

Apart from what you will glean from scanning the articles themselves, at the front or the back of the journals you will find a page of information for authors. This will vary greatly in its comprehensiveness. There will always be basic information such as formatting details for the typescript like spacing, style of references, need for an abstract, key words, preferred length, etc. There will most likely be, as we mentioned, some statement relating to the scope of articles the journal accepts and the submission and review procedures. Be advised of the time the review process sometimes takes. This can commonly be six months, although one top general education journal pledges to give a decision within six weeks. The proportion of articles rejected by some journals can be considerable, as can the time to publication once the article has been accepted. These measures generally increase with the prestige of the journal; the first can vary from virtually none rejected to as many as 90% rejected and the latter from almost immediate publication to well over a year.

Equally well, the nature of the content of the articles accepted by journals varies. For many professional journals, and some less prestigious academic referred journals, an interesting, well written and structured, relatively straightforward account of the methodology and findings will be acceptable. As a general rule a top-level academic referred journal will, apart from the obvious relevance/interest for the readership and a sound empirical base, be looking for a research report with either an original theoretical perspective or an illuminative analytical framework (and, of course, quality in all other respects).

Using literature

We considered in Chapter 5 four different types of literature that you may want to use in your research and as a consequence perhaps cite in your writing: research reports, methodological texts, theoretical accounts and literary works. In a simple research report, such as the one outlined above, a very limited amount of literature would characteristically be cited and, in the main, it would detail the findings of previous research in the area. One of the central characteristics that differentiate professional, pedagogic and academic modes of writing is the use of literature. As a very general rule the more prestigious the journal, the more extensive the literature bases of the articles it publishes. You would not overall, however, expect to find even the more erudite of articles referenced as extensively as pedagogic writing, such as an academic thesis.

Characteristically, your article would begin with a review of the literature relating to the area. There is no need to leave this to the writing-up stage to complete; we suggested in Chapter 5 that as you read articles and books you should be making notes about the central features of the methodology/findings/theoretical argument, etc. It is from these notes that you will be able to construct a review of the literature relating to the area of your interest. Literature can also be used to effect if it is threaded through as an integral part of the account rather than all presented in an initial review. Key quotations could be employed throughout to buttress the argument or you could develop a dialogue between two opposing perspectives from the literature, perhaps resolving the dilemma in a 'third way' of your making.

We recommended in Chapter 5 ways in which you could identify appropriate quotations and included in the resources for research are instructions as to how you should cite them in the text and reference them in the bibliography. Quotations, if they are small, can be put in inverted commas and inserted in the text but, as a rule of thumb, if they are about four lines/forty words in length it is customary to indent them. In order to keep the quotation brief you may need to cut phrases/sentences from it, in which case you should replace them with ellipses.

An alternative approach to using literature involves taking a particular theoretical framework as a lens through which to read the data. Be imaginative in your search for sources of ideas: they do not have to be that original, just used in a different context for a different audience.

Illustration: taking a particular theoretical framework

Foucault has a lot to say about the way that 'discourses' (e.g. OFSTED, National Numeracy Strategy) and power within society position people in particular ways. Jones and Brown (2001: 719) use Foucault's ideas to effect when interpreting play activity in a 'kitchen homebase' in a nursery classroom:

> the girls were not willing to be passive participants in the play. Melissa, for example, tries to take some of the dough that the boys had been 'cooking' with. This prompts

> Nathan to declare: 'No they're not cooked.' Furthermore, he uses a loud and firm voice and in doing so perhaps lends authority to his role as 'cook'. His tone of voice reminds the children, particularly the girls, that as cook it is he who has the knowledge and thus the power to decide when the pies are cooked.

Another example would be McNamara *et al.* (2002) who employed a contemporary anthropological lens to talk about initial teacher training in England. They saw it not as a linear progression but as a complex process of 'in-between-ness' that involved the performance of symbolic acts and the undertaking of 'ritual ordeals'. In particular, the article explored the most recently imposed 'ritual ordeal', the Numeracy Skills Test.

Illustration: using an anthropological lens

A trainee teacher describes how she prepared herself physically and psychologically for the day ahead. This is followed by the authors' reflections:

> It was just . . . getting up in the morning, getting dressed, putting on something [so] that I looked like somebody, doing my hair and then struggling with the books and the briefcase and all the things that I need for the day . . . and then from that point when they came in, in the morning and said good morning and I took the register, that's when I felt like a teacher (final year trainee).

> Here we have examples of the symbols that signify teacher status. The sartorial appearance of the ceremonial robes: getting dressed to look like 'somebody', 'doing my hair'. The canticles and responses prescribed in the rites: verbal refrains associated with teaching/learning behaviours such as 'good morning everyone', 'good morning Miss Smith'. The wielding of instruments of surveillance such as 'taking the register' and, finally, 'books' and 'briefcase': the symbols of power and knowledge often subsumed in myth/ritual (McNamara *et al.*, 2002: 871).

The process of writing

Writing is a very personal pursuit and being prescriptive can be difficult, although Chesebro (1993) displayed no such reluctance in his article, 'How to get published'. He commenced his list of recommendations with 'write', making the case that, in order to be published, it is necessary to engage in certain physical behaviours and, in particular, writing: words, sentences, paragraphs and pages. This advice is not as trite as it may seem – as you will remember we strongly recommended that you should not wait until your project is done and dusted to begin writing up. Write continuously from the outset: notes about your methods, readings, diary entries, musings, quotes, data, etc., will be a sound foundation on which to start constructing your report or article. Chapter 6, you will recall, gave you some suggestions about the writing of research diaries. Chesebro recommends devising a 'rigorous writing schedule' and, indeed, many writers (and academics) would claim that they need to set aside quality time of considerable length to make any progress, whilst others can make do quite adequately with a snatched hour or so here and there.

'Be willing to be criticised' is another of Chesebro's tenets and, although we would not express it in such stark terms, it is an issue that requires consideration. If you submit an article for publication you will receive feedback, which sometimes can be quite harsh and perhaps painful (even when the reviewer likes it!). Generally speaking the more prestigious a journal you aim for, the more rigorous the review process. Articles submitted to professional journals are not formally peer reviewed – a process that defines academic journals – but they are subjected to editorial scrutiny, to a greater or lesser degree. So when you submit your writing do so with the mindset that it is just 'another draft'; don't get so attached to each comma and apostrophe that you can't bear even to think about restructuring it for resubmission. Although a few people write fluently in perfectly formed sentences, most writers go through an extensive process of drafting and redrafting before they attain a satisfactory product. Looking on the positive side, peer reviews offer valuable personal advice on writing style, research methodology, literature, etc., but don't be too surprised if, in the case of two reviewers, they completely disagree.

The important message to take from this is don't be put off: even the most highly acclaimed academics have their work roundly condemned from time to time; the criticism is not about you, it is about the writing, so don't take it personally. Indeed, what we are going to suggest next is perhaps more threatening: ask a friend or colleague to read your work in its early drafts and to give you some informal feedback. Ask for general comments but also be specific on the features of the writing that you want feedback on. We talked in Chapter 7 about using your critical community during the earlier phases of the research and it is just as important at this stage to use that relationship.

Pen-portraits: an alternative genre of writing

We discussed pen-portraits as an analytical tool in Chapter 8 and there are many reasons why they are an attractive and useful form of data management and reporting. This is particularly so in your situation as a practitioner, perhaps reporting on practices within your own institution and/or classroom. The approach involves using data from semi-structured interviews with teachers, or perhaps pupils, to produce a vignette of a particular individual in respect to a specific aspect of his or her biography or role. The abridged pen-portrait below is one developed as part of a longitudinal study of trainee teachers that followed them from entry into the course to their first year in teaching.

Illustration: mathematics – a victory narrative fought in three phases?

For 19-year-old Helen school mathematics was about 'numbers and how they work'. It required very particular attributes: 'you had to be committed . . . to sit there and work out the problems . . . have patience to not give up half way through.' Helen saw the pursuit of victory as a lonely and demanding personal crusade: 'I like a place where I can get somewhere on my own, and just keep going until I get there . . . you've got to be able to work it out on your own because if someone does it for you, you might be able to get the answer but you don't know how you got there.'

Junior school mathematics 'was easy, there was no algebra and calculators with lots of buttons . . . it was just plain, simple text books . . . you progressed through to the next level and wanted to get better because you would get a better colour book than your friend had'. The competition didn't always go Helen's way, however. There had been at least one major defeat in these early days: Helen 'could never get the hang of' tables which 'everyone else used to do really fast'. It was a failing that she attributed to lack of effort on her part.

Secondary school saw the emergence of the 'scientific calculator' and 'scary words', like 'sine' and 'cosine'. Salvation was at hand, however, in the form of a really good mathematics teacher who 'always explained everything very clearly and took time if you couldn't do it to go over it step by step'. Victory was again assured: 'you tackled and you understood it, you could just do exercise after exercise and get them all right and it was a good feeling being able to do it.' The 'working out was important' but getting the 'right answer was the best thing, getting the whole exercise right was really good'. Helen again used to 'like maths a lot', even 'algebra . . . shocking, but I felt really good'.

That's not to say there weren't still minor skirmishes, 'times when I just couldn't work out how to get what x equalled and when you went wrong and you'd done a whole, long sum and you get a different answer to everyone else and you just can't understand where you went wrong'. Disillusionment set in, however, when Helen failed to get her coveted grade A at GCSE; she had 'thought she was really good' and even 'considered doing it to A level'. But now Helen was embarking upon a new phase of the campaign, that of becoming a teacher of mathematics.

The idea of fictionalising pen-portraits is less well established; it is based on methodological approaches developed by Bolton (1994) and Campbell and Kane (1998). We discussed in Chapter 8 how analysis of interviews of teachers or pupils could be achieved with a view to developing a set of ideal typical characters that are representative of the amalgams of characteristics, views, opinions and experiences of the interviewees. By creating fictional characters in this way, it is possible to use verbatim reports and anecdotes from a number of different sources to produce lively, authentic accounts to facilitate easy access to the research data. One major advantage of fictional pen-portraits is that they maintain the anonymity of individuals; even in a relatively large secondary school this may be an issue – for example, it would be quite common for there to be only one female religious education teacher. An abridged version of a fictional pen-portrait, developed as part of a baseline survey of CPD in which the authors were involved, is shown below. It concerns Julia, who is aged 30 and has been teaching in a small rural secondary school for four years.

Illustration: a baseline survey of CPD

CPD to me is about advancing my skills, keeping up to date with current developments, finding new ways of teaching, using resources. I've been here four years. I'm the history department basically. I started off in PR then worked with adults with learning difficulties for about three years, that's what got me interested in teaching really. I try to keep updated but don't go on that many courses, the problem is time really, with all the stuff you have to get on with every day. And the government ICT training has annoyed me, it was a complete and utter waste of time. Compared for example with one ICT course I went on and what made that great was that he was a historian and a classroom teacher you could use it with the children. You felt you had learnt something new, and it wasn't just 'sharing ideas' – that's another thing that annoys me there was one history course that was absolutely appalling no ideas, no materials. I feel very strongly that someone delivering a course shouldn't be relying on the audience to be part of the delivery.

The best training days are the ones when you have time to prepare or go on the net, there's so much good stuff there. We also had OFSTED a couple of years ago and the training was all about getting through, which in all fairness focused me into making sure I was on target. But it's difficult for me on my own, in a small school like this. I think it's a lot better in maths because they seem to have more going on there are more of a close-knit community. I have to rely on things like the history group which meets once a term in the LEA. Also I had a student this term and she's been good, bringing ideas.

What's interesting is that the CPD co-ordinator has been pretty good when I've asked about going on courses, but he's never come to me with any suggestions. Within this school I feel very much if you're interested that's fine but it's another question whether they are interested in you. So it's not that management aren't supportive when you ask for something but you need extra responsibilities at my level to develop your management skills and there's not much room for development for me at the moment. And to be honest I'm not prepared to lose out on having a life . . . in fact I'm not really sure I will stay with the job.

Such materials, apart from being a vehicle through which to report research, were planned in this project as a professional development resource. They were intended to stimulate discussion of CPD between heads, CPD co-ordinators and teachers, to help them understand the complexity of the dynamic relationship between factors such as school culture and structures, national/school priorities, performance management, planned career development, etc. Using this approach can allow the voices of staff to be heard anonymously, and in a non-confrontational way, through issues rather than personalities. Some of the issues for discussion arising from the vignette above might relate to themes such as:

- Time and, implicitly, workload – Julia felt too busy to engage in CPD.

- Perceptions of CPD – Julia had a traditional notion of CPD as courses/conferences, etc.

- Key features of successful CPD – for Julia this was applicability in the classroom.

- Key features of unsuccessful CPD – for Julia this was 'sharing ideas' courses.

- 'Training' – ICT training got a particularly bad press.

- School culture – Julia as the only history teacher in the school felt isolated.

- Watching and talking with colleagues – Julia had little opportunity.

- School management of CPD – Julia felt the co-ordinator was not proactive enough in providing systematically planned opportunities.

- Personal career management – Julia sees no clear career pathway. It is hard work and frustrating and she doesn't know if the rewards are sufficient.

Concluding remarks

In this chapter, we have considered at length some of the genres of writing you may adopt when reporting your research and identified some key issues with regard to the use of literature, the writing process itself and getting published. As our journey through the processes and practices of practitioner research draws to a close we will move on to consider the final stages of (self-) evaluation and dissemination. Writing up, and even publishing, is not synonymous with dissemination although it is well on the way. You may consider if you get as far as writing up, as we very much hope you will, that your work is done – that you have completed your academic dissertation and received your award, or submitted the report on research you were commissioned to do for your employer. Yet your work may have implications for others and you will undoubtedly have expended a lot of time and effort on it, too much to allow it to be wasted! You need to ensure that your work gets an airing; you cannot rely upon the people that need to know finding out about it, you must be proactive in the dissemination process. Additionally, as we mentioned earlier, it is often only when you distance yourself from your work by articulating it to others, or writing things down, that you begin to evaluate what you have done – ask yourself those difficult questions! In the final chapter, we shall now consider these issues in more detail.

Further reading

Altrichter, H., Posh, P. and Somekh, B. (1993) *Teachers Investigate their Work*. London: Routledge.

A very useful guide to action research methods for beginning researchers in education and the social sciences. In particular, it has a useful chapter on 'Making teachers' knowledge public'.

Bell, J. (1999) *Doing your Research Project*. Buckingham: Open University Press.
This immensely popular research methods reader again contains a useful chapter on 'Writing the report'.

Campbell, A. and Kane, I. (1998) *School-based Teacher Education: Telling Tales from a Fictional Primary School*. London: David Fulton.

11 Evaluating and Disseminating Research

OVERVIEW

As we mentioned in Chapter 1, Lawrence Stenhouse (1975) defined research as 'systematic inquiry made public'. The last two words of this definition indicate the importance of disseminating research. The ostensible process for making research public is that of peer review or evaluation by submitting findings either orally or in print through publication. It is only in the last 30 or so years that educational research has had substantial funding and has therefore been more widely reported in the public domain. It is really only in the last ten or so years that practitioner researchers have had opportunity to do so. It follows, therefore, that practitioner researchers are fairly new to dissemination and the processes of peer review and evaluation. Thus teacher researchers should seize every opportunity to share practice and developments with other practitioners and to influence and shape policy at classroom, school, local and national and international levels.

The professional agenda

From the outset of the design of a research topic or project, it is useful to consider the opportunities for evaluation and dissemination in order to prepare strategies. Mortimore (1991: 228) provides a useful list to consider before publication, some of which will be pertinent to practitioner researchers and the arena in which they wish to disseminate. He advises early identification of opportunities; awareness of and preparation for controversies which may arise from the findings; consultation with 'stakeholders' in the research; and recommends the use of an advisory group or critical community.

Before disseminating one's research, one should evaluate that research. The level of sophistication of the evaluation will depend on the stage of the research. In the early stages evaluation may be tentative. Towards the end things should have hardened up. Evaluating research provides evidence of rigour, reliability and transparency of approach. There is a variety of ways ranging from self-evaluation and peer evaluation to more formal external evaluation processes undertaken by funding bodies or councils or by people from other institutions, such as universities. In consideration of self-evaluation and monitoring of small-scale practitioner research projects, a number of the following ideas should help and support researchers and are well worth considering.

The evaluation and dissemination that you are being urged to undertake should be honest about disasters and modest about triumphs. It should share doubts and inconsistencies and recognise ambivalences. At its freshest it will contain anecdotes told against oneself. Above all, as practitioner engagement it will, hopefully, draw frequently upon material that reveals the actions and responses of children and participants woven in and out. Teachers will most certainly be interested in how the pupils have responded, so make sure the evaluation and dissemination recognise and do not lose sight of why the research is being undertaken and the perspectives of the pupils.

Care must be taken to make the processes of evaluation and dissemination accessible in two ways. It should be comprehensible in respect of the language used: resist the temptation to parade a mastery of new research jargon that you might have picked up. It should also be published where teachers can hear it, read it and find it. It is an irony of some traditional research that, although it may be about teachers' practice or children's performance and published in journals or forums of albeit high standing, it is rarely visited by teachers themselves. Practitioner research hopefully brings with it a new philosophy of dissemination. Therefore, please note the 'health warning' before proceeding to consider the practicalities of dissemination.

If you are still in doubt about how to adopt a suitable tone or find a suitable mode of presentation, look inwards. All evaluation should start with the 'self'. What sort of things do you and your colleagues like to hear about? Remember these need not be at the heart of your research. They could quite simply be interesting by-products but will make your presentations, in whatever form, more living and real.

You could certainly come up with your own list but it may be useful to draw upon the Campbell and Jacques (2003) study of teachers setting out their expectations and subsequently reporting and evaluating their interim findings. This small group of 19 teachers had expectations of improvement in pupil performance, a generic term with several subcategories of meaning.

Slightly less than half the teachers in the study expected an improvement in pupil behaviour and in pupil collaborative skills. About a quarter expected their pupils to have a better understanding of the learning process and to acquire specific knowledge or skills. A small number of teachers expected improvement in communication skills or a change in pupil attitude to the subjects they were being taught.

Other individual responses from teachers about impact on pupils identified the following expectations:

◆ An improvement in concentration.

◆ Longer time to be spent on task.

◆ Improved access to the curriculum.

◆ Greater pupil responsibility for their own behaviour.

◆ Increased pupil awareness and self-evaluation.

From the above list and from the detail of the responses, it was evident that most teachers responding expected that the research project would impact on pupils in some or all of the following ways: more engagement in learning; higher achievement in the subject; and an increase in subject knowledge with some impact on social and learning skills. Many of the teachers were expressing hopes and aspirations because they were not exactly certain what really to expect: they anticipated an upward turn in everything rather than focused outcomes relating to their particular research.

That is the road on which these practitioner researchers set out. It constitutes, we would argue, an 'agenda of interest' which you could bear in mind when telling your own story. It is worth repeating that these issues may be tangential to your research, but helpful reminders to you of the sorts of things that engage an audience of teachers. Many will say 'Well that's all very well, but what actually happened?' This is where honesty of reporting matters, and presenters win their audiences through triumphs of serendipity. Again we have an 'agenda of interest', perhaps an even more interesting one. The majority of teachers in the study reported improvement in teaching as follows:

- A better clarity of what was being taught.

- More pupil-centred planning for teaching.

- Focused evaluation.

- More appropriate classroom routines.

- Being more aware of the use of praise.

- Giving pupils more time to think.

- Developing more focused teaching strategies.

- Having more specific objectives and targets for teaching.

- Making more careful observations of pupils.

- Enabling reflection and questioning about teaching.

- Adapting and changing teaching strategies and trying different ones.

A quarter of teachers in the study reported improvements in a better team spirit in school and more opportunities for learning about learning. Possibly they were thinking of their own team spirit. A smaller number of teachers reported outcomes which were more specific and would not constitute an 'agenda of interest'.

About a third of teachers in the study reported a rise in pupil attainment and an increase in pupils' perceptions of their own skills and self-awareness. Evaluation indicated that it had been more difficult than first imagined to find real evidence of the raising of pupil achievement.

Having spent some time on what we would argue is a 'professional agenda' that you should always have as a frame of reference when evaluating and subsequently disseminating, it is now time to look more closely at the mechanics.

The mechanics of evaluation

Evaluation of research should report honestly on progress and whether the research has met its initial aims and objectives. It should address the effectiveness, worth or value of the research project. It may be timely to revisit some aspects of qualitative and quantitative issues for discussion. Not all research seeks to *measure* outcomes or phenomena. It may be appropriate to *illustrate* or *illuminate* outcomes or phenomena for interpretation or for interrogation by the profession or critical community in order to further the knowledge or understanding in the area of research.

The evaluation of your research might answer some of the following questions:

- ◆ What are understood to be the outcomes of the research?

- ◆ How do these relate to the aims and/or objectives of the research?

- ◆ What can be identified as the effectiveness, impact or influence of the research?

- ◆ How can the effectiveness, impact or influence be illuminated, illustrated or measured?

- ◆ Who has critically appraised the research?

- ◆ How has this critical appraisal been integrated into the research process?

In order to self-monitor and self-evaluate, a number of strategies can be employed.

Learning aid: self-monitoring and self-evaluation

The seven most common strategies for self-monitoring and self-evaluation:

1. The keeping of a research diary that documents the conduct of the research project in dated entries is, as we have explained earlier, a key tool for your

research. One of the matters you should keep under close scrutiny is the consideration of whether the project has kept to the initial brief. If not, why not?

2. The keeping of a log of the changes, dilemmas and problems and the resolution of these will also help your evaluation. There should be plenty of scope here for the 'warts and all' approach advocated earlier.

3. Where possible give regular, brief, oral or written interim reports on the progress towards objectives to your mentor, tutor or critical friend. Remember the concept of critical friend is an intellectual concept to be explored in detail (see Chapter 7) rather than a social diversion.

4. You should give consideration regularly to whether sufficient, relevant and appropriate literature has been consulted. Chapter 5 gives advice on how to consult and review literature to support and enhance your argument and case.

5. Be sure to review regularly your research methods and whether they are appropriate for the study. Do not remain locked into the predetermined pattern simply because that is what you committed yourself to in the beginning. Flexibility is a key feature of research.

6. As findings emerge and as you collect data, give consideration as to whether the data you are acquiring are robust and of good quality.

7. Try to construct, either by oneself or with a critical friend or community, a set of searching questions for evaluation purposes.

Certainly for practitioner research, good evaluation practice should contain an element of peer evaluation. When thinking about peer evaluation there are a number of ways of approaching the involvement of others. In more informal situations the following strategies would contribute to, or make use of, peer evaluation. Consider enlisting one of the following:

◆ A critical friend.

◆ A critical community group.

◆ A colleague or co-researcher in own or other school or LEA.

- ◆ A local adviser or advisory teacher.

- ◆ A mentor or tutor at university if enrolled on a course or research degree or being mentored.

- ◆ A network contact from Classroom Action Research (CARN) or a local variety set up by practitioner researchers.

The value of having a peer involved in evaluation is dependent upon his or her ability to connect with the topic or area being researched. Collegial exchange and discussion of the detail of a project enable concrete and precise language to be used and shared. Researchers may choose a peer with specialist knowledge of their area in order to gain more depth in their study. Alternatively, a person who has little knowledge of the area but who is an experienced researcher may offer different viewpoints and perspectives on the research in progress. Checking out the research with others can significantly enhance the process and the findings. However, as in the discussion in Chapter 7 on critical friendship, peer scrutiny and collaboration, steps have to be taken to ensure that undue influence is not exerted on the researcher and the research project by peer evaluators.

The role of the peer evaluator could be to undertake some of the following:

- ◆ Asking questions about the research process and progress.

- ◆ Acting as a 'sounding board' for developments.

- ◆ Being a source of questions about why certain decisions have been taken.

- ◆ Providing feedback on research plans and interim reports.

- ◆ Liasing with other researchers and projects which could facilitate comparison.

- ◆ Providing a different perspective to challenge thinking and actions.

The degree of informality in the context of monitoring and evaluation will be dependent on the style, scale and scope of the research being undertaken and the relationships formed between researcher and peer evaluator. Often in small-scale practitioner research projects, the pattern is for informal arrangements. Care should be taken to ensure that the relationship does not become too cosy and that there is sufficient challenge in the evaluative exchanges and interactions as well as support.

It would be as easy to conduct this peer review by email, telephone and fax, or through a discussion room on a website, as it would be to meet on a regular basis. Many networks already exist and are on the increase as initiatives such as educational action zones, Excellence in Cities, Beacon schools and training, technology and specialist schools all develop and start to look for partners and peers to share their ideas with and to help them develop and evaluate their plans.

More formal types of peer review could be obtained through publication of 'research in progress' for in-house or professional journals. There is a clear difference between the two. In-house journals are generally much less formal and often anxious for copy. The 'house' you are in might be no more than your own school, possibly your local cluster. It might be a regular LEA bulletin. Most universities have scope for publishing details of local teachers' work, particularly if those teachers are registered on courses at advanced level.

However, a professional journal is more formal, but not normally to the level of formality of needing academic 'referees'. Where referees are used, good practice is to feed back their comments and these naturally help to serve as evaluatory comments. Alternatively, an editorial board may give evaluative feedback. Responses from peers should be welcomed. Do not shy away from being put in a position of being criticised. Provided you read the criticism as constructive, it should always help.

Another approach is the presentation of interim findings or research in progress at seminars for discussion and debate. Once again, do not be shy about seeking and finding such opportunities. Your own staffroom is probably as good a place to start as any. Provided you do not concentrate on telling people how clever you are (see earlier warning) there is every chance of a sympathetic hearing. Other potential sources of seminar presentations will again be clusters, networks, LEAs and local universities.

It can hardly be overstressed how important it is that you share your research work. Disseminating your research has become very much more significant as increasing numbers of practitioners are engaging in classroom and school-based research. There is also more recognition of the connection between action research and practitioner research and professional development and the need to learn from others who have successfully harnessed research to promote professional development.

However, as we explained earlier, engaging in research into your own practice and professional development is a risky business and can mean exposure of your unsuccessful initiatives as well as the successful ones. This said, we agree with Elliott's (1991) view that early, practitioner action research projects like the Humanities Curriculum Project, the Ford Teaching Project and the Teacher–Student Interaction and the Quality of Learning Project significantly enhanced the professional development of the teachers involved in them. This was especially true where teachers were 'in the lead' and had ownership of the design and conduct of the research and when they were able to tolerate the inevitable loss of self-esteem when being observed and researched by colleagues. Elliott (1991: 35) maintains that: 'in order to adopt an objective attitude to their practice, teachers need to be able to tolerate the existence of gaps between their aspirations and practice, with a consequent lowering of their self-esteem.' More recently, Campbell (2002), in her exploration of research and the professional self, found that teachers' participation in a research project: 'had had a significant effect on their professional lives . . . For some it has meant a long hard slog to see the light at the end of the tunnel; for others while not quite equating to a "Damascus" type of experience, it has certainly resulted in enlightenment.'

The culture in schools, in groups of schools, in educational action zones and similar project and initiative groupings is changing to be more collaborative and collegial, as evidenced by Day (1999: 175) who refers to 'networking through partnerships' as an important learning mode, and can also be seen in the proliferation of action learning sets or groups in schools. The recent English CPD Strategy (2001) promoted 'schools as learning communities' and provided opportunities for teachers to become funded researchers. Explicit in this strategy is the emphasis on dissemination of good practice through collaboration and collegial exchange.

Learning aid: disseminating good practice

You may find it helpful to think that ways of disseminating practitioner research at various levels can be achieved through a 'ripple effect'. You might like to think of it as follows:

◆ Tell the staff/your department via an oral presentation.

◆ Develop or contribute to a school newsletter.

◆ Circulate a written account to staff.

◆ Tell other schools in your cluster/network in similar ways.

◆ Inform your LEA, and maybe get them to provide a forum for you and others like you.

◆ Tell your local subject association/professional group or professional association, many of whom have individuals with issue and subject development and research personnel and interests. Give an oral or written report or write an article.

◆ Tell the wider versions of these associations (for example, submit an article to *History Today* or *Nursery World*).

◆ You could use the medium of *The Times Educational Supplement* by writing a letter or short article, with a contact/email address for correspondence.

So far we have given consideration to issues of disseminating whilst remaining safely within a practitioner/professional context. You could be more ambitious. You could go beyond professional journals and submit an article to a nationally refereed journal. A refereed journal has a set of guidelines for potential contributors that state the conventions and 'rules' for submission of articles. Examples can be found, amongst many others, in the *British Educational Research Journal* (*BERJ*), the *Education Action Research Journal* (*EARJ*) or the *European Educational Research Association Journal*. The editor or editorial board (mainly UK based) will send submissions to experienced people in the research area who will referee them – that is, read them and assess their quality and recommend whether the articles should be accepted as they stand, or amended in some minor or major way for resubmission, or whether they should be rejected. It would be sensible to seek some advice from university tutors or other researchers who have published in these journals or to seek mentoring support if you are unfamiliar with procedures. A useful strategy is to team up with someone else. Co-writing and joint publication between new and experienced researchers are an option to explore, especially if you are engaged in a master's or research degree programme.

Most universities run seminar programmes for researchers and these can be useful meeting places for gaining advice or finding research partners. People at such seminars can explain to you what opportunities exist to publish or present. So be bold. After all, as a practitioner you are already deeply into disseminating as part and parcel of your practice. Present a paper to a conference, either individually or, as described above, in collaboration with a colleague researching in the same area, or with a mentor or more experienced researcher. There are many conferences ranging from professional, subject conferences to international, wide-ranging gatherings. As with journals, some conferences are refereed and select papers against rigorous assessment criteria but others favour a wider participation approach. Conference organisers and committees produce guidelines for presenters which help you to write a paper that would be acceptable (for conference information, see: http://www.leeds.ac.uk/educol).

By now you are an experienced disseminator. You have also discovered that if you have something to say there are people who wish to pay attention. Your morale is high, so seek to progress further. Tell the wider world via international journals. Writing for an international audience requires a different perspective from writing for a local or national one. An international journal will have an editorial board that comprises international experts in the field covered by the journal and the standard of research will need to meet very rigorous and high-level criteria and, of course, the research will have to be of interest to an international audience. Much inquiry about journals and the type of articles previously published would be necessary before submission. However, once again, support, mentoring and co-writing are strategies that could prove to be useful at this stage. Times are changing too. Whereas international journals have largely been forums for traditional research rather than practitioner research, *Educational Action Research* is an international journal that wishes to publish more practitioner research in the future.

Perhaps it is time to come down from the rarefied academic heights and return to more mundane practicalities. Much of what has been alluded to lies within established procedures. Yet new traditions are emerging by which you can tell people about your research.

Tell the Internet through the school website, LEA website, mentoring university website, the DfES research website (or even your own website). Tell your mentoring or tutoring university organisation through their website, action research networks, research forums, conferences, in-house journals, dissertations or assignments. Search out like-minded people on the Internet, through the *TES*, through your neighbouring university and through correspondence.

Make a video or CD-ROM. Naturally it helps if your material is visually stimulating. Moreover, there is expense involved but perhaps you have planned, have been well informed and have obtained funds which would help you fund the making of CD-ROMs and video tapes. Find opportunities for poster sessions. Many conferences invite less experienced researchers to present a poster for informal discussion. These sessions provide a supportive environment for beginner researchers. A poster is constructed which summarises the research you are doing and identifies some discussion points and issues. This you display in some conference assembly point or thoroughfare. Most of the time you stand by it and engage in discussion with interested colleagues as they pass by.

Concluding remarks

As we noted earlier, there is a tendency for much practitioner research, but especially small-scale action research which is designed to improve an individual's practice, not to see the light of day. This is perhaps understandable, but we believe it is important that even research which is highly specific to a particular situation should still at least be shared within the wider context that provides a setting for that situation. It is for that reason that we close our contribution to this book by suggesting ways in which you might wish to share your findings, if only to encourage others to carry out research which we believe to be absolutely necessary for practice to develop in ways that are informed by research, rather than to ossify into a kind of unthinking, unreflective behaviour which, over time, will lose whatever force it once had.

Resources for Research

Harvard referencing: questions and answers

As a rule of thumb you should bear in mind that your aim is to give the readers the information they will need to find for themselves all the quotations and references that you have used. Note that you can use either underlining or italics (as here) but not both.

1. How do I make reference to a quotation from a book? In your essay you would write:

(Austin, 1955: 26)

and in your references section you would translate this as:

Austin, J.L. (1955) *How to Do Things with Words*. Oxford: Oxford University Press.

2. How do I make reference to a quotation from an article in a journal where there are more than two authors? In your essay you would write:

(Cooper *et al.*, 1977: 248)

and in your references section you would translate this as:

Cooper, W.E., Eimas, R.D. and Corbitt, J.D. (1977) 'Some properties of linguistic feature detectors', *Perceptions and Psychophysics*, 13(2): 247–52.

3. How do I make reference to an article in an edited collection of papers? In your essay you would write

(Hirst, 1970: 113)

and in your references section you would translate this as:

Hirst, P.H. (1970) 'What is teaching?', *Journal of Curriculum Studies*, 13(1) (reprinted in his edited *Knowledge and the Curriculum*, London: Routledge & Kegan Paul, 1974, 101–15).

4. How do I make reference to a quotation (for example, from Handy) that I have found in another source (for example, in Slee) but have not read in the original myself? In your essay you would write:

(Handy, 1989, cited in Slee, 1992: 89)

and in your references section you would translate this as:

Handy, C. (1989) 'Missing ingredients', *The Times Higher Education Supplement*, 10 March: 26 (cited in Slee, P. (1992) 'Apocalypse now? Where will higher education go in the twenty-first century?', in P.W.G. Wright (ed.) (1990) *Industry and Higher Education*. Buckingham: Open University Press, 88–92).

5. How do I make reference to an anonymous report? In your essay you would write:

(Anon, 1991: 39)

and in your references section you would translate this as:

Anon (1991) *Singapore Polytechnic FY 91 Annual Report*. Singapore: Singapore Polytechnic Press.

6. How do I make reference to quotations from someone who has written two pieces in one year (for example, in a newspaper), especially in the case of 'Anon'? In your essay you would write:

(Anon, 1993a: 30)

and in your references section you would translate this as:

Anon (1993a) 'Time for government to license and control education agencies', *The Straits Times*, 10 April: 30.

Later you might have to cite another piece from the same paper, so you would have to write in your essay:

(Anon, 1993b: 30)

and in your references section you would translate this as:

Anon (1993b) 'What if Caucasian who punched me and damaged car leaves the country?', *The Straits Times*, 10 April: 30.

Notice that in your references you have to list the 'Anons' in chronological order so that Anon (1991) will come before Anon (1993a). The same applies to a named author who might have published more than one piece in his or her lifetime, so you would also put their publications in chronological order.

7. How do I make reference to a quotation from an essay or dissertation which has not been published? In your essay you would write:

(Roche, 1992: 1)

and in your references section you would translate this as:

Roche, C. (1992) 'My own reflection on learning.' Unpublished paper for the Diploma/MEd course, Sheffield University and Singapore Polytechnic, 11 December.

8. How do I make reference to material in the modules? In your essay you would write:

(Clough, 1992: 20)

and in your references section you would translate this as:

Clough, P. (1992) 'My own learning', Module 1, Unit 2, *Understanding Learning and the Learner*. Sheffield: Sheffield University Division of Education Press, 10–20.

9. How do I make reference to a source written in a different language? In your essay you would write:

(Untersteiner, 1949)

and in your references section you would translate this as:

Untersteiner, M. (1949) *Sofisti, Testimonianze e frammenti (The Sophists)*. Turin: Turin University Press.

10. How do I present a long quotation in my text? Unlike ordinary short quotations (where you would use quotation marks and allow the material you are quoting from to fit smoothly within your own text) longer quotations need to be presented differently. You need to indent from the left, use single space and you do *not* use quotation marks. Such a quotation in your essay would look like the example below.

Example: quoting a lengthy extract

. . . and so we do in fact need 'carefully controlled empirical research' (Hirst, 1970: 101). However, it is clear that there are many different types of research.

In education:

> the essentially practical, problem-solving nature of action research makes this approach attractive to practitioner-researchers who have identified a problem during the course of their work, see the merit of investigating it and, if possible, of improving practice (Bell, 1987: 5).

We now need to examine this popular form of research and see how it can apply in my country.

11. How do I reference material I have taken from the Internet? In your essay you would write:

(Vann, 1994: 20)

and in your references section you would translate this as:

Vann, A.S. (1994) 'Curriculum and textbooks: a happy marriage?', *Principal*, 73(4): 20–1, National Association of Elementary School Principals, Reston, VA (online – http://www.enc.org/reform/journals/ENC2410/2410.htm – accessed 18/10/00).

12. How do I reference a personal communication? In your essay you would write:

. . . the event structure. It has been suggested (Green, pers. comm., 1997) that a new type of information may need to be added . . .

You do not need to include anything in the references section for personal communications unless there is some extra essential information you need to add.

When you have completed your work you need to construct your references section.

Learning aid: constructing your references section

When constructing your references list, bear the following points in mind:

1. Every author you have used must appear here

2. in alphabetical order of surname

3. with initials (not first or personal names)

4. followed by the earliest year the reference was published.

5. If you have used more than one piece of this author's work you have to use chronological ordering (see question 6 above).

6. You must provide full details of the references used.

7. Italicise (or underline – when you underline text this is meant to indicate to a typesetter that the text should be italicised) book, journal and newspaper titles.

8. Do not italicise or underline the titles of articles in books, journals or newspapers.

9. Single spacing, with a single blank line between references.

10. If possible, use a hanging indent (where the second line is not against the margin) as this makes it easier to read your references.

Example: completed references section

Anon (1991) *Singapore Polytechnic FY 91 Annual Report*. Singapore: Singapore Polytechnic Press.

Anon (1993a) 'Time for government to license and control education agencies', *The Straits Times*, 10 April: 30.

Anon (1993b) 'What if Caucasian who punched me and damaged car leaves the country?', *The Straits Times*, 10 April: 30.

Austin, J.L. (1955) *How to Do Things with Words*. Oxford: Oxford University Press.

Clough, P. (1992) 'My own learning', Module 1, Unit 2, *Understanding Learning and the Learner*. Sheffield: Sheffield University Division of Education Press, 10–20.

Cooper, W.E., Eimas, R.D. and Corbitt, J.D. (1977) 'Some properties of linguistic feature detectors', *Perceptions and Psychophysics*, 13(2): 247–52.

Handy, C. (1989) 'Missing ingredients', *The Times Higher Education Supplement*, 10 March: 26 (cited in Slee, P. (1992) 'Apocalypse now? Where will higher education go in the twenty-first century?', in P.W.G. Wright (ed.) (1990) *Industry and Higher Education*. Buckingham: Open University Press, 88–92).

Hirst, P.H. (1970) 'What is teaching?', *Journal of Curriculum Studies*, 13(1) (reprinted in his edited *Knowledge and the Curriculum*, London: Routledge & Kegan Paul, 1974, 101–15).

Roche, C. (1992) 'My own reflection on learning'. Unpublished paper for the Diploma/MEd course, Sheffield University and Singapore Polytechnic, 11 December.

Untersteiner, M. (1949) *Sofisti, Testimonianze e frammenti (The Sophists)*. Turin: Turin University Press.

Vann, A.S. (1994) 'Curriculum and textbooks: a happy marriage?', *Principal*, 73(4): 20–1, National Association of Elementary School Principals, Reston, VA (online – http://www.enc.org/reform/journals/ ENC2410/2410.htm – accessed 18/01/00).

Summary report from the Friars Primary School: 'Improving Literacy: Intervention for Low-achieving Pupils'

AIM

To devise teaching strategies to improve the literacy of low-achieving pupils at Key Stage 2.

BACKGROUND

This research was set in an inner-city area of great social deprivation. The school intake is characterised by high pupil mobility, 63% uptake of free school meals (three times the national average) and one third of the pupils on the special needs register. Poor phonological awareness and the need to develop oral language skills were identified by Ofsted (1998) as action points. The improvement of literacy standards was a high priority in the school development plan.

SUMMARY OF FINDINGS

- ◆ Ability to decode polysyllabic words is a critical skill at reading age 8 +.

- ◆ Individual test results can be unreliable – long-term trends are more valuable.

- ◆ Humour is an important motivating factor and an aid to memory.

- ◆ Active engagement in poetry through performance is a valuable teaching medium.

- ◆ Short-span focused tasks improve motivation and increase time on task.

- ◆ Focus on spelling increases the capacity for phonic and reading skills.

- ◆ Children of low ability respond well to challenging work if it is appropriately presented.

- ◆ Children of low ability respond well to oral group work and it leads to solid learning outcomes.

RESEARCH DESIGN

The Year 5 class was selected as being in particular need of attention. A skills audit was conducted on the class: reading tests identified 17 low-achieving pupils (reading age less than chronological age); phonological awareness tests were carried out on the 17 project children; and self-esteem and non-verbal reasoning tests were given to the whole class. The project children were split into two roughly equivalent groups (A and B) for teaching purposes and an intensive booster programme, equivalent to a daily one-hour lesson over a four-week period, was delivered to each group in turn. The pupils were interviewed at the end of the booster programme and their reading age changes recorded. The research aimed to monitor the differential effectiveness of the literacy booster programme in raising reading standards. A secondary focus of the research was to question how informative and reliable these tests were when compared with teacher assessment in identifying learning difficulties and assessing pupil performance. The main problem areas identified in the pupil skills audit and by teacher observation were:

- decoding of polysyllabic words;

- low vocabulary level;

- poor phonological awareness;

- deficiencies in short and long-term memory; and

- rhyme recognition, awareness of pitch and sense of rhythm.

Non-verbal reasoning

The N-VR test (NFER) was cheap and relatively quick and easy to administer and as an overall indicator of ability it was a useful guide against which to measure progress in reading. The correlation between N-VR and reading age was marked and indicated no particular evidence of underachievement. A small number of results did, however, seem unreliable – e.g. one child with an RA of 10.6+ and three other children with an RA of 8+ achieved no score in the N-VR test. One statemented child of very low ability with a reading age of 6.4 did, however, score. The table below shows the distribution of N-VR scores for the whole class.

N-VR score	No score	74–79	80–84	85–89	90–94	95–99	100–4	105–9	110–4	115–9
Project	3	1	3	4	3	2				
Non-project	1		1	2	5	1	2	1	2	2

Self-esteem

The self-esteem test (Harter-Anglicised version standardised in Scotland) didn't throw any particular light on the project children's reading ability. Analytically it included six categories: scholastic, social, athletic, appearance, behaviour (whether the child saw him or herself as well or badly behaved) and global (an overall measure). The girls in the class as a whole showed a fairly standard distribution, the project girls appearing to demonstrate no particular pattern of response except in scholastic performance where 8 out of 11 had a lower-than-average opinion of themselves. The boys in the class as a whole had in general much poorer opinions of themselves than average. With respect to athletic competence and scholastic ability none scored above average and for social acceptance only two boys scored notably above average. If any pattern was apparent in project/non-project children the former had a slightly higher opinion than the others of their athletic competence and their physical appearance. The test was done with adult support: the brighter children were in small groups and the less able individual. Yet there was evidence that some of the results were unreliable: a few children appeared to have ticked the boxes in a particular pattern down the page and in other cases the responses were apparently contradictory.

Phonological awareness

The PhAB test (NFER) identified six specific areas of phonological difficulty. It was administered individually (25 minutes per child) to all project children and the results were scored and collated. Some 11 out of the 17 children scored in one or more categories. Two children of exceedingly low ability scored higher than the ones whom staff had previously identified as having phonological problems.

TEACHING PROGRAMME

An intensive course of 20 lessons each of 50 minutes duration comprising four components:

1. phonics

2. spellings

2. sentence construction

2. poetry and performance.

The phonics component focused on a different group of word endings each week. Each lesson started with a list of around 30 words that were discussed, decoded and their meanings explored:

week 1: endings that say 'ur': -er, -ar, -or, -our
week 2: endings that say 'us' and 'shus': -us, -ous, -ious, -cious, -tious, -scious, -xious
week 3: endings that say 'shun' and 'zhun': -tion, -sion, -ssion, noting that many of these words have the same second-last syllable, eg. -ation, -iction, -ension, -ision, etc.
week 4: endings in y: -y, -ly, -ity, -vity, -arity, -icity, plus revision of all endings.

Three words from the weekly list were written down each day for four days as spelling homework. On day five of each week there was a spelling test. Words from the list were combined in sentences, first orally then in written form, the more outrageous the better: 'Mrs Jennings is ancient but decent, different and intelligent.' 'Paul's feet are odorous.' 'Are you a criminal? What if I am – it's personal!' 'Mrs Jennings is glorious and not hideous or tedious.' The hard work of sentence writing thus became fun.

The final part of each lesson entailed studying a poem (one per week) and practising it for performance to another class. Poetry was chosen because it provided a short, manageable and complete piece of text and also because the children found it enjoyable to practise and reread repetitively. Poems were selected for their humour and interesting content; their strong sense of rhythm and regular rhyme patterns; and because they contained a reasonable number of polysyllabic words from target lists and other new vocabulary. They included *The Shark* by Lord Alfred Douglas, sections I and III of *Night Mail* by W.H. Auden and *Macavity, the Mystery Cat* by T.S. Eliot.

MAIN FINDINGS

The programme overall did what it set out to do. In the three (four for group B) months preceding the programme the children made reading progress at approximately one third of the speed of the average child, but in the month of the booster programme they made four times the expected monthly progress of the average child. All reading ages were tested using the Salford Sentence Reading Test. The tables below show the reading progress of the 16 project children over a period of 18 months.

Group A NAME	N-VR 20/4/98	RA 20/1/98	Change in RA in 3 months Jan to April	Change in RA during May booster	RA July 98	RA Jan 99
S C	97	9.0	+0.4	+1.2	10.0	10.6+
D H	92	7.6	+0.2	−0.3	7.1	8.3
S H	85	10.0	0	0	10.6	10.6
L Z	74	6.5	−0.1	+0.4	6.7	7.0
L B	94	8.3	0	+0.7	8.1	9.3
A H	88	9.2	+0.2	+0.4	9.8	10.6
N T	89	9.0	+0.4	+0.4	9.8	Left
M W	95	8.2	0	+0.2	8.3	8.7
Average monthly change per pupil			up 1/2 month per month	up 4 months per month	up 5/6 month per month	

Group B NAME	N-VR 20/4/98	RA 20/1/98	Change in RA in 4 months Jan to May	Change in RA during booster June/July	RA July 98	RA Jan 99
S B	86	8.4	+0.3	+0.7	9.20	Left
P E	80	9.0	0	+0.6	9.60	9.2
R B	94	8.3	−0.4	+1.0	8.11	8.1
D C	n/s	9.0	0	+0.6	9.60	9.8
L E	80	8.1	−1.0	+0.9	9.30	9.1
K F	80	8.1	+0.4	+0.8	9.70	9.3
N G	n/s	9.8	+0.2	+0.8	10.60	10.6+
L R	n/s	8.1	+0.1	+0.9	8.11	9.0
Average monthly change per pupil			up 1/5 month	up 4 months	down 1/5 month	

All reading ages are given in years and months (e.g. 9.11 means 9 years 11 months).

SOME EXAMPLES OF TYPICAL RESPONSES FROM THE CHILDREN

- ◆ 'The sentences were really funny and weird ones'; 'we had a laugh about it when we called each other'

- ◆ 'I like Macavity it's dead funny'; 'they clap and laugh at the end of it'

- ◆ 'First we came in the group and I kept rushing through the words and getting them wrong now I am splitting them up and getting them right'

- ◆ 'Practices and trying to make the words and split them all up and when you split them up you say . . . like operation op-er-a-tion just split them up'

- ◆ 'We've been missing our experiments cause we are doing volcanoes and we are going to make them erupt. I wanted to do it . . . but I guess my spelling is more important'

Further reading

Byrne, B. (1998) *The Foundations of Literacy: The Child's Acquisition of the Alphabetic Principle*. Hove: Psychology Press.

Crystal, D. (1996) 'Language play and linguistic intervention', *Child Language Teaching and Therapy*, 12 (3): 328–44.

Johnston, S. and Watson, J. (1999) 'Reading'. *Literacy and Learning*, April/May.

McGuinness, D. (1998) *Why Children Can't Read*. London: Penguin Books.

SOEID (1996) *Methods of Teaching Reading: Key Issues in Research and Implications for Practice. Interchange* 39.

References

Altricher, H., Posh, P. and Somekh, B. (1993) *Teachers Investigate their Work: An Introduction to the Methods of Action Research*. London: Routledge.

Ball, S. and Goodson, I.F. (eds) (1985) *Teachers' Lives and Careers*. London: Falmer Press.

Bassey, M. (1995) *Creating Education through Research: a global perspective of educational research for the 21st century*. Newark: Kirklington Moor Press in conjunction with the British Educational Research Association, 1995.

Beach, R. (1987) 'Differences in autobiographical narratives of English teachers, college freshmen and seventh graders', *College Composition and Communication*, 38(1): 56–69.

Blunkett, D. (2001) ' Foreword', in *Learning and Teaching: A Strategy for Professional Development*. London: DfES.

Bolam, R. (1999) 'The emerging conceptualisation of INSET: does this constitute professional development?' Paper presented at the Annual Conference of the Standing Committee for the Education and Training of Teachers, 26–28 November, GEC Management College, Rugby.

Bolton, G. (1994) 'Stories at work: fictional-critical writing as a means of professional development', *British Educational Research Journal*, 20(1): 55–68.

Bolton, G. (2001) *Reflective Practice: Writing and Professional Development*. London: Paul Chapman.

Bullough, R.V., Knowles, J.G. and Crow, N.A. (1991) *Emerging as a Teacher*. London: Routledge.

Campbell, A. (2000) 'Fictionalising research data as a way of increasing teachers' access to school-focussed research', *Research in Education*, 63: 81–8.

Campbell, A. (2002) 'Research and the professional self', in O. McNamara (ed.) *Becoming an Evidence-based Practitioner: A Framework for Teacher Researchers*. London: RoutledgeFalmer.

Campbell, A. and Jacques, K. (2001) 'Best practice researched: an investigation of the early impact of teacher research on classrooms and schools.' Paper presented at the Annual Conference of British Educational Research Association, Leeds University, 13–15 September.

Campbell, A. and Kane, I. (1998) *School-based Teacher Education: Telling Tales from a Fictional Primary School*. London: David Fulton.

Campbell, A. and Kane, I. (2000) 'Best of times, worst of times: the importance or otherwise of regular in-servicing', *Teacher Development*, 4(2): 293–302.

Chesebro, (1993) 'How to get published', *Communication Quarterly*, 41(4): 373–82.

Clandinin, D.J. and Connolly, F.M. (1995) *Teachers' Professional Knowledge Landscapes*. New York, NY: Teachers' College Press.

Clandinin, D.J. and Connolly, F.M. (1996) 'Teachers: professional knowledge landscapes: teachers' stories – stories of teachers – school stories – stories of schools', *Educational Researcher*, 25(3): 24–30.

Cochran-Smith, M. and Fries, M.K. (2001) 'Sticks, stones and ideology: the discourse of reform in teacher education', *Educational Researcher*, 30(8): 3–14.

Connolly, F.M. and Clandinin, J. (1990) 'Stories of experience and narrative enquiry', *Educational Researcher*, 19(5): 2–14.

Costa, A.L. and Kallick, B. (1993) 'Through the lens of a critical friend,' *Educational Leadership*, 51: 49–51.

Cumming, C. (1982) 'A first try: starting the day', in G. Payne and E. Cuff (eds) *Doing Teaching*. London: Batsford Studies in Education.

Dadds, M. (1995) *Passionate Enquiry and School Development: A Story about Teacher Action Research*. London: Falmer Press.

Dallat, J., Moran, A. and Abbott, L. (2000) 'A collegial approach to learning and teaching as the essence of school improvement', *Teacher Development*, 4(2): 177–98.

Day, C. (1993) 'Reflection: a necessary but not sufficient condition for professional development', *British Educational Research Journal*, 19(1): 83–93.

Day, C. (1999) *Developing Teachers: The Challenges of Lifelong Learning*. London: Falmer Press.

Denzin, N. (1970) *Sociological Methods: A Source Book*. London: Butterworths.

Denzin, N. (1985) *Interpretive Biography*. London: Sage.

DfES (2000) *Professional Development: Support for Teaching and Learning*. London: DfES.

DfES (2001) *Learning and Teaching: A Strategy for Professional Development*. London: DfES.

Ebutt, D. (1985) 'Educational action research: some general concerns and specific quibbles', in R. Burgess (ed.) *Issues in Educational Research*. London: Falmer Press.

Edwards, A. and Collinson, J. (1996) *Mentoring and Developing Practice in Primary Schools: Supporting Student Teacher Learning in Schools*. Milton Keynes: Open University Press.

Edwards, A., Gilroy, P. and Hartley, D. (2002) *Rethinking Teacher Education: Collaborative Responses to Uncertainty*. London: RoutledgeFalmer.

Egan, G. (1990) *The Skilled Helper: A Systematic Approach to Effective Helping* (4th edn). Pacific Grove, CA: Brooks/Cole.

Eisner, E.W. (1978) 'The impoverished mind', *Educational Leadership*, 35: 615–23.

Elliott, J. (1974) *Implementing the Principles of Inquiry/Discovery Teaching*. Norwich: CARE Publications, University of East Anglia.

Elliott, J. (1981) *Action Research: Framework for Self-evaluation in Schools. TIQL Working Paper* 1. Cambridge: Cambridge Institute of Education.

Elliott, J. (1991) *Action Research for Educational Change*. Buckingham: Open University Press.

Elliott, J. (1999) 'Evidence-based practice, action research and the professional development of teachers.' Paper presented at the Manchester Metropolitan University Staff Development Day, May.

Elliott, J. (2001) 'Making evidence-based practice educational', *British Educational Research Journal*, 27(5): 555–74.

Eraut, M.E. (1994) *Developing Professional Knowledge and Competence*. London: Falmer Press.

Eraut, M.E. (1999) 'Preface', in C. Day (ed.) *Developing Teachers: The Challenges of Lifelong Learning*. London: Falmer Press.

Fueyo, V. and Koorland, M.A. (1997) 'Teacher as researcher: a synonym for professionalism', *Journal of Teacher Education*, 48: 336–44.

Garet, M.S., Porter, A.C., Desimone, L., Birman, B.F. and Yoon, K.S. (2001) 'What makes professional development effective? Results from a national sample of teachers', *American Educational Research Journal*, 38(4): 915–45.

Gilroy, D.P. (1993) 'Reflections on Schön: an epistemological critique and a practical alternative,' in D.P. Gilroy and M. Smith (eds) *International Analyses of Teacher Education*. Oxford: Carfax Press.

Graham, J. (1999) 'From welfare to the knowledge based economy', in J. Graham (ed.) *Teacher Professionalism and the Challenge of Change*. Stoke-on-Trent: Trentham Books.

Habermas, J. (1972) *Knowledge and Human Interest*. London: Heinemann.

Hardy, B. (1986) 'Towards a poetics of fiction' in *Novel: A Forum*. Providence, RI: Brown University Press.

Hargreaves, A. (1992) 'Foreword', in A. Hargreaves and M.G. Fullan (eds) *Understanding Teacher Development*. London: Cassell.

Hargreaves, A. (1994) *Changing Teachers, Changing Times: Teachers' Work and Culture in the Post-modern Age*. New York, NY: Teachers' College Press.

Hargreaves, D. (1997) 'In defence of research for evidence-based teaching: a rejoinder to Martyn Hammersley', *British Educational Research Journal*, 23: 405–19.

Hay McBer (2000) *Research into Teacher Effectiveness: Phase 11 Report: A Model of Teacher Effectiveness*. London: DfEE.

Hitchcock, G. and Hughes, D. (1989) *Research and the Teacher: A Qualitative Introduction to School-based Research*. London: Routledge.

Holly, M.L. (1988) 'Reflective writing and the spirit of enquiry', *Cambridge Journal of Education*, 19(1): 71–80.

Holly, M.L. (1989) *Writing to Grow: Keeping a Personal-professional Journal*. Portsmouth, NH: Heinemann.

Hopkins, D. (1985) *A Teachers' Guide to Classroom Research* (1st edn). Buckingham: Open University Press.

Hopkins, D. (1993) *A Teachers' Guide to Classroom Research* (2nd edn). Buckingham: Open University Press.

Hoyle, E. (1974) 'Professionality, professionalism and control in teaching', *London Review*, 3(2): 121–36.

Hustler, D., Cassidy, T. and Cuff, T. (eds) (1986) *Action Research in Schools and Classrooms*. London: Allen & Unwin.

Hustler, D., McNamara, O., Jarvis, J., Londra, M., Campbell, A. and Houson, J. (2003) *Teachers' Perceptions of Continuing Professional Development*, DfES Research Report 429. London: DfES.

Jones, L. and Brown, T. (2001) '"Reading" the nursery classroom: a Foucauldian perspective', *Qualitative Studies in Education*, 14(6): 713–25.

Joyce, B. and Showers, B. (1982) 'The coaching of teaching', *Educational Leadership*, 40(2): 4–10.

Kennedy, J. (1996) 'Starting points', *Action Researcher*, 5: 21–4.

Kuhn, T.S. (1961) 'The function of measurement in modern physical science', in H. Woolf (ed.) *Quantification, A History of the Meaning of Measurement in the Natural and Social Sciences*. Indianapolis, IN: Bobs Merrill.

Lewin, K. (1947) 'Frontiers in group dynamics: concept method and reality in social sciences', *Human Relations*, 1(1): 5–41.

Lewin, K. (1948) *Resolving Social Conflicts*. London: Harper & Row.

Little, J.W. (1982) 'Norms of collegiality and experimentation: workplace conditions of school success,' *American Educational Research Journal*, 19: 325–40.

MacBeath, J. (1999) *Schools Must Speak for Themselves: The Case for School Self-evaluation*. London: Routledge.

Macdonald, J. (1986) 'Raising the teacher's voice and the ironic role of theory', *Harvard Educational Review*, 56: 355–78.

Macintyre, C. (2000) *The Art of Action Research in the Classroom*. London: David Fulton.

Maclure, M. (2001) 'Arguing for your self: identity as an organising principle in teachers' jobs and lives', in J. Solar *et al.* (eds) *Teacher Development: Exploring our own Practice*. London: Paul Chapman.

Magee, B. (1973) *Popper*. Glasgow: Fontana.

Maynard, T. and Furlong, J. (1993) 'Learning to teach and models of mentoring', in D. McIntyre *et al.* (eds) *Mentoring: Perspectives on School-based Teacher Education*. London: Kogan Page.

McIntyre, D. and Hagger, H. (1993) 'Teachers' expertise and models of mentoring', in D. McIntyre *et al.* (eds) *Mentoring: Perspectives on School-based Teacher Education*. London: Kogan Page.

McNamara, O., Hustler, D., Stronach, I., Beresford, E., Botcherby, S. and Rodrigo, M. (2000) 'Room to manoeuvre: mobilising the "active partner" in home–school relations', *British Educational Research Journal*, 26(5): 473–89.

McNamara, O., Roberts, L., Basit, N.T. and Brown, T. (2002) 'Rites of passage in initial teacher training: ritual, performance, ordeal and the numeracy skills tests', *British Educational Research Journal*, 28(6): 861–76.

McNiff, J., Lomax, P. and Whitehead, J. (1996) *You and Your Action Research Project*. London: Routledge.

Mortimore, P. (1991) 'The front page or yesterday's news: the reception of educational research', in G. Walford (ed.) *Doing Educational Research*. London: Routledge.

Newman, S. (1999) *Philosophy and Teacher Education: A Reinterpretation of Donald A. Schön's Epirtemology of Reflective Practice*. Aldershot: Ashgate.

Nias, J. (1989) *Primary Teachers Talking: A Study of Teaching as Work*. London: Routledge.

Nixon, J. (ed.) (1981) *A Teacher's Guide to Action Research*. London: Grant McIntyre.

Pawson, R. (1989) *A Measure for Measure*. London: Routledge.

Popper, K. (1971) 'Conjectural knowledge: my solution to the problem of induction', in *Objective Knowledge*. Oxford: Oxford University Press.

Popper, K. (1974) in *Conjectures and Refutations* (5th edn). London: Routledge & Kegan Paul.

Powell, J. (1985) *The Teacher's Craft*. Edinburgh: Scottish Council for Research in Education.

Ruddock, J. (1991) *Innovation and Change*. Buckingham: Open University Press.

Russell, T. and Munby, H. (1991) 'Reframing: the role of experience in developing teachers' professional knowledge', in D.A. Schön (ed.) *The Reflective Turn*. New York, NY: Teachers' College Press.

Sachs, J. (1999) 'Using teacher research as a basis for professional renewal', *Journal of Inservice Education*, 25(1): 39–53.

Schön, D.A. (1983) *The Reflective Practitioner: How Professionals Think in Action*. New York, NY: Basic Books.

Sikes, P., Measor, L. and Woods, P. (2001) 'Critical phases and incidents', in J. Solar *et al.* (eds) *Teacher Development: Exploring our own Practice*. London: Paul Chapman.

Simpson, M. and Tuson, J. (1995) *Using Observations in Small-Scale Research*. Edinburgh: The Scottish Council for Research in Education.

Smyth, J. (1987) *Educating Teachers: Changing the Nature of Pedagogical Knowledge*. Lewes: Falmer Press.

Smyth, J. (1991) *Teachers as Collaborative Learners*. Buckingham: Open University Press.

Somekh, B. (1995) 'Analytical methods', *Academic Development*, 1(1): 65–7.

Stenhouse, L. (1975) *An Introduction to Curriculum Research and Development*. London: Heinemann Educational.

Stenhouse, L. (1980) 'Product or process: a response to Brian Crittenden', *New Education*, 2(1): 137–40.

Stoll, L. and Fink, D. (1996) *Changing our Schools*. Buckingham: Open University Press.

Strauss, A. and Corbin, J. (1998) *The Basics of Qualitative Research: Techniques and Procedures for Developing Grounded Theory*. Thousand Oaks, CA: Sage.

Thomas, D. (1995) 'Treasonable or trustworthy text: reflections on teacher narrative studies', in D. Thomas (ed.) *Teachers' Stories*. Milton Keynes: Open University Press.

Tomlinson, J. (1997) 'Foreword', in M. Thompson (ed.) *Professional Ethics and the Teacher*. Stoke-on-Trent: Trentham Books.

Tomlinson, P. (1995) *Understanding Mentoring*. Milton Keynes: Open University Press.

Tripp, D. (1993) *Critical Incidents in Teaching: Developing Professional Judgement*. London: Routledge.

Walford, G. (ed.) (1991) *Doing Educational Research*. London: Routledge.

Whitty, G. (1999) 'Teacher professionalism in new times.' Paper presented at the Annual Conference of the Standing Committee for the Education and Training of Teachers, Dunchurch, Rugby, 26–28 November.

Wilkin, M. (1992) *Mentoring in Schools*. London: Kogan Page.

Winter, R. (1988) 'Fictional critical writing: an approach to case study research by practitioners and for in-service work with teachers', in J. Nias and Groundwater-Smith (eds) *The Enquiring Teacher*. London: Falmer Press.

Woods, P. (1993) *Critical Events in Teaching and Learning*. London: Falmer Press.

Woods, P. (1994) 'Adaptation and self-determination in English primary schools', *Oxford Review of Education*, 20(4): 387–410.

Wragg, E.C. (1999) *An Introduction to Classroom Observation* (2nd edn). London: Routledge.

Wragg, E.C. Wikeley, F.J., Wragg, C.M. and Haynes, G.S. (1996) *Teacher Appraisal Observed*. London: Routledge.

Index

academic mode, of writing 170
accountability 13, 14, 15, 29
action learning sets 195
action research 24, 25, 26, 44, 45, 81, 132, 194, 195
actions, recording 89–90
agenda of interest 189, 190
aims of research, in reports 174
alerting services 74
analytical commentaries 37–8
analytical memos 134, 135
anonymous reports, referencing 200
anthropological lens 180
appraisal 20, 22
assumptions 5, 6–7
ATHENS 76
attitudes, exploring 30, 32, 116–17
audiences, research 32, 169–72, 197
authenticity 84, 118
autonomy *see* licensed autonomy; professional autonomy

background to research, in reports 175
Bath Information and Data Services (BIDS) 75, 76–7
BEI *see* British Education Index
beliefs, exploring 30, 32, 116–17
BERA *see* British Education Research Association
bias 83, 84, 101
bibliographic databases 75, 76–8
bibliographic indexes 75, 76–8
bibliographic referencing systems 67–8
bibliographic software packages 71
bidding, culture of 15
BIDS *see* Bath Information and Data Services
biographical pen-portraits 142–3
biographies 91–2
Blunkett, David 16
books
    literature reviews 78
    recording details 68–9

British Education Index (BEI) 75, 76
British Education Research Association (BERA) 54, 74, 87, 99, 107
British Library 73, 74

CARN *see* Collaborative Action Research Network
categories
    conceptual 131
    creating 133
    descriptors 153–4
    developing 133–5
category response questions 148–51
CD-ROMs 198
central control, of teaching profession 16
CERUK *see* Current Educational Research in the UK ›
challenge
    critical community 118
    critical friendship 110, 115
    for development 107
chapters, recording details of 69
charitable foundations 75
Chart Wizard 165–6
chartered teachers 15
classroom observation 94
closed questions 99, 102
closed response questions 148
co-inquiry 123
co-writing 196
coaching 107
coding
    qualitative data analysis 130–2
    quantitative data management 148–59
coding strips 150
collaboration 41, 88, 106, 107, 122
Collaborative Action Research Network (CARN) 107
collaborative cultures 122
collaborative research 24, 25
colleagues

importance of relationships with 16
informal interviews with 35–6
involving in research 85, 106
see also critical friends
collegial discussion 106, 107, 193
commentaries, informal interviews 40–1
commercialisation, of education 29
commonsense tradition 3–7
communication, critical community 120–1
communities of practice 123
competing agendas, professional development 15
conceptual categories 131
conceptual frameworks 88
conceptualisation, teacher education 14
conference proceedings 54
conferences, presenting papers to 197, 198
confidentiality 84, 88–9, 99, 110, 121, 172
confrontation, for development 107
context
    contextualist tradition 7, 8
    for observation 97–8
    see also political context; social context
contextualist tradition 7–9, 10, 126, 128
continuing professional development
    baseline survey of 18
    CPD strategy 14, 195
    fictional pen-portrait 183–5
    funding 20
    lack of autonomy 47
    recognition of importance 14
control
    research questions and design 25
    teaching profession 16
conversations 101
copyright 172
core features, professional development 18–19
counselling interviews 100
CPD *see* continuing professional development
craft knowledge 26
crises, professional identity 29
critical appraisal 122
critical community 118
    collaborative cultures 122
    colleagues as members of 85
    communication 120–1
    illustrations 119–20
    organisation 121–2
    role of 85, 120, 121

validation of research 108, 110
critical friends
    colleagues as 85
    informal interviews with 36–7, 41
    qualities to look for 111
    role of 106–7, 109
    skilled helper model 112
    as supervisors x
    as trusted persons 115, 117
    typical questions asked by 113
critical friendship
    basis of 106–7
    examples 114–17
    how it works 109–10
    issues and friendship qualities 110–11
    in research methodology 108
    role 85
    starting 109
critical incident analysis 89–90
critical incidents 45
critical pedagogy 108
critical reflection 25
criticality 25
criticism 181, 194
cross-checking, research 85
culture of inquiry 26
Current Educational Research in the UK
    (CERUK) 75
curriculum development 9
curriculum discussions 108
curriculum vitae (CVs) 18, 33–5, 92

data analysis 83–4
    from interviews 102
    methodological texts 66
    qualitative 125–44
    quantitative 159–64
data collection 81, 82f, 83, 146, 175
data management, quantitative 148–59
data presentation 164–8
Data Protection Act (1998) 172–3
data subjects, rights 173
databases
    bibliographic 75, 76–8
    for managing literature 71
deduction 3, 4f, 5, 6, 127
democratic professionalism 16
deregulation, teaching profession 16

descriptive statements, qualifying 137
descriptors, to categories 153–4
designs *see* research designs
DfES 54, 57, 74, 75, 123
dialogue 41
diary interviews 100
diary keeping 32, 43–6, 88–90, 114
dilemma analysis 140–1
disclosure 107
Discourse on the Positivist Spirit 3
dissemination of research 188, 195–8

Economic and Social Research Council (ESRC) 75
education, commercialisation 29
education journals 73
education theory and practice 66
Educational Action Research 197
educational action zones 195
educational research *see* research
electronic journals 73–4
electronic resources xi, 74–6
End Note 71
ePolitix 75
ERIC 76
error eliminations 7, 8f, 9
ESRC *see* Economic and Social Research Council
ethical codes 87
Ethical Guidelines (BERA) 87, 99
ethics 81, 84, 88–9, 121, 172–3
ethnographic interviews 100
Europe, professional development 14
evaluation
    of research 83–4, 176, 188, 191–5
    see also self-evaluation
evidence, recording 89–90
Evidence for Policy and Practice Information (EPPI) Centre 75
evidence-based policy 5
evidence-based practice 24, 25
expectations, of interim findings 188–9
experts, critical community 118
external evaluation 188

feasibility 84
feedback 107, 108, 181–2
fictional critical writing 45–6, 92, 93
fictional pen-portraits 142–3, 183–5

field notes 94, 129
findings
    in research reports xii, 176
    reviewing 79
    writing up 174–5
    see also interim findings
force field analysis 43
foreign languages, referencing sources 201
formal evaluation 188
frame of references 7, 8, 190
frequencies, calculating 159–63
Friars Primary School, summary report from 205–10
funding 20, 24, 25, 123

General Teaching Council (GTC) 16, 54, 74, 75
generalisations 7, 8
genres, research writing 169–72
good practice, disseminating 195–8
government policy, professional development 14
grounded theory 128
group interviews 101
GTC *see* General Teaching Council

Harvard System 68, 199–204
Hay McBer Report 20
health warning, dissemination of research 188
higher education personnel, importance of 26
hypothesis testing 3, 4f, 5, 127

identifying research topics 49–51
identity *see* professional identity
image-based records 173
image-based research 66
impact of research 189–90
in vivo codes 131, 132
in-house journals 194
in-service education 47
index systems 68–71
induction 3, 4f, 5, 7, 127
inequalities, provision for development 15
inference 97
informal interviews 36–7
    analytic commentaries 37–8
    commentaries 40–1
    questions
        for constructing 37
        for eliciting information 39–40

informal participant observation 93–4
informality, monitoring and evaluation 193
information gateways 75, 76
information response questions 151–2
initial teacher education and training 29, 123
Initial Teacher Training Partnership 71
innovation overload 47
inquiry
   challenges of 41–2
   process of 7, 8f
   teacher-initiated 25–6
   see also co-inquiry; narrative inquiry; systematic
     inquiry
insiders 94
institutions, web-based sources 74
interim findings
   expectations of 188–9
   presentation of 194
Interlibrary Loan Scheme 73
international audiences, writing for 197
Internet
   access to xi
   disseminating research 197
   referencing material from 202
interpretation, of data 129
interrogating data 136–7
interventionist policies 25
interviews 98–102
   analysing data from 102
   bias 101
   confidentiality 99, 173
   formats 100–1
   planning and preparation 98–9
   questioning 99–100
   tactics 101–2
   tape recording 129
   see also informal interviews

joint publication 196
Joseph Rowntree organisation 75
journal articles
   databases 76
   recording details of 70
   referencing 199
journal catalogues 73–4
journals
   peer reviews 194
   writing for 177–8, 196, 197

journals (diaries), keeping 32, 43–6, 88–90, 114

knowledge 3, 4f, 5, 6, 7, 10, 26, 41, 44
knowledge creation process 108

language 128
learning communities 14, 16, 26, 51, 55–6, 121,
     122, 123, 195
learning support assistants 108
*Learning and Teaching: A Strategy for Professional
     Development* 14, 16
legal considerations, research writing 172–3
libraries xi, 71–2
library catalogues 72–3
licensed autonomy 15–16
life histories, importance of 35
life history interviews 100
Likert scale 96, 153, 163
list response questions 152–3
literary works 67
literature 65–79
   managing 67–71
   in research reports 178–80
   reviewing 78–9
   searching for 71–8
   types of 65–7
literature searches
   problems with 54–6
   research reports 175
log of events 32, 90
'logic of discovery' 128
'logic of verification' 128
loneliness, of researchers 106

master teachers 107
mean scores, calculating 163–4
measurements, scientific research 127
media interest, teachers and teaching 28
mentoring 106, 108, 110, 122–4, 197
meta-metaphors 139
metaphor analysis 138–40, 141
methodological texts 66
Microsoft Access 71
Microsoft Excel 151, 160–6, 167–8
Microsoft Word 71, 151, 166
modular material, referencing 201
motivation x

narrative 91
narrative inquiry 30
National College of School Leadership (NCSL)
    121, 123
National Curriculum 13, 14, 22, 29, 108
National Foundation for Educational Research
    (NFER) 74, 75
national testing 13
NCSL *see* National College of School Leadership
negative cases 135, 136
networked learning communities (NLCs) 14, 51,
    55–6, 121, 123
networking 122, 195
networks
    action research 197
    peer review 194
    teacher learning 22, 23, 26, 52, 85, 118
    teachers, pupils and parents 16
new managerialism 29
new public management 29
newspapers
    sources 74, 75
    writing for 177
NFER *see* National Foundation for Educational
    Research
nil responses 159
non-computerised records 173
noticings 95

objective knowledge 3, 4f, 5, 6
objectivity 94, 126, 195
observation 5, 7, 8, 93–8, 108
open coding 131–2
open ended questions 99, 102
open response questions 126, 157–9
opportunities, SWOT analysis 42
oral history interviews 100
organisations, web-based sources 74
outcomes of research 191
outcomes-based view, of education 24
ownership
    of research 172
    of teaching 13

paper copies, journal articles 70
partnerships 16, 23, 26, 52, 85, 118, 195
pattern analysis 141
pedagogic mode, of writing 170

peer evaluation 188, 192–3
peer evaluators 193
peer review 22, 85, 106, 107, 194
peer scrutiny 106, 107, 109, 110
pen-portraits 91
    analysis 142–4
    illustration 38–9
    research reports 182–6
    sharing 32–3
    writing 36
performance management 20, 29
performance management review 47
personal 60–1
personal communication, referencing 202
personal data 173
personal dimensions, teachers' lives 29
personal index systems 68–71
pie charts 165–7
political context, research and development 13–17
Popper, Karl 7, 8, 116
positivist tradition 3–7
posters 198
practitioner research 24, 26, 61, 80, 104
    dissemination of 188, 195–6
    methods 81–3
principles, professional development 17
problems in research
    contextualist tradition 8
    identifying topics 51
    positivist tradition 5–7
professional agenda 187–90
professional associations 75
professional autonomy 20, 22–4, 25, 29, 47
professional codes of practice 94
professional development ix, 12–26
    element of choice in 47
    exploring personal 30–5
    mentoring 122–3
    political context 13–17
    principles 17, 18
    professional autonomy 22–4
    reflection 41
    teacher researchers 24–6
    types of activity 18–20
        interrogating value of 20–1
professional identity 28–47
    exploring professional development 30–5
    image of teachers and teaching 28–30

telling your story 35–46
professional journals 194
professional knowledge 10
professional landscapes 92
professional mode, of writing 170
professional practice 1
professionalism 16–17, 23, 32
professionality 32
project descriptions, research reports 175
pseudo-scientific methodologies 128
publication, writing for xii, 177–8, 196
pupil achievement
    discussions 108
    raising 15, 190
pupils
    expected impact on pupils 189
    response to evaluation and dissemination 188
purposes, research writing 169–72

qualitative research 2
    authenticity 84–5
    data analysis 125–44
    observation 95
    subjectivity 94
qualities, critical friends 111
quantitative research 2
    data collection 127
    observation 95, 96
    viewed as only legitimate research 25
    see also questionnaires
quantity response questions 151–2
questionnaires 146–68
    data analysis 159–64
    data management and coding 148–59
    data presentation 164–8
    legal and ethical considerations 173
    small-scale 144, 147
    using 102–4
questions
    critical friends might ask 113
    for identifying research objectives 56–9
    informal interviews
        for constructing 37
        for eliciting information 39–40
    in interviews 99–100
    for reflective writing 87–8
    for research designs 83
    for writing pen-portraits 36

quotations 179
    referencing 199, 200–3

'raising standards' agenda 14, 15, 22, 25, 28
ranking response questions 156–7
rating scale response questions 153–6, 163
rating scales 96
reality 3, 4f
refereed journals 196
referees 194
reference sections
    constructing 203
    example of completed 204
referencing systems 67–8, 199–204
reflection
    challenges of inquiry 41–2
    insufficiency in itself 41
    in research reports 176
reflection-in-action 10
reflection-on-action 10
reflective practice 9–10
reflective practitioner 9, 10, 87
reflective writing 87–8
*The Reflective Practitioner: How Professionals Think
    in Action* 10
relevant research, locating 65–6
reliability 84
replication studies 66
reporting research 169–86
    describing research process 175–6
    genres, purposes and audiences 169–72
    legal and ethical considerations 172–3
    pen-portraits 182–6
    process of writing 181–2
    using literature 178–80
    see also research reports
representation 84
research
    consequences of xii
    disseminating 195–8
    evaluation, mechanics of 191–5
    literature see literature
    methodologies 66, 81–3
    professional agenda 187–90
    reporting 169–86
        format 174–5
        genres, purposes and audiences 169–72
        legal and ethical considerations 172–3

pen-portraits 182–6
process of writing 181–2
research process 175–6
using literature 178–80
resources for 199–210
stages 83–4
techniques 87–104
  biography, stories and fictional critical
    writing 91–3
  interviewing 98–102
  observation 5, 7, 8, 93–8
  questionnaires 102–4, 146–68
topics
  concluding remarks 62–4
  identifying 49–51
  individual ways of approaching 60–2
  literature searches 54–6
  research objectives 56–60
  scale of the proposal 52
  timelines 53
traditions 1–10
  contextualized approach 7–9, 10, 126, 128
  positivist approach 3–7
  quantitative and qualitative approaches 2
  reflective practice 9–10
see also practitioner research; qualitative
    research; quantitative research
research designs
  control over 25
  questionnaires 102–4
  questions for 83
research participants, rights 83, 173
'research in progress' 194
research reports
  format 174–5
  of other projects 65–6
  for publication 177–8
researchers
  loneliness of 106
  teachers as 9, 22, 24–6
resources
  for research 199–210
  see also electronic resources
responsibilities, research participants 83
results see findings
rights, research participants 83, 173
ripple effect, dissemination of research 195–6
risks, in research 194–5

SARA 74
scale of research 52
Schön, Donald 9, 10
school culture 195
school improvement 23
school self-evaluation 22
schools, as learning communities 195
scientific research 3, 85, 127
Scotland, professional development 14–15
Scottish Council for Education Research 74
search strategies 77
selection, in research 94
self-determination 23–4, 47
self-esteem 195
self-evaluation
  by teachers 25, 30, 47, 188, 191–2
  schools 22
self-monitoring 25, 191–2
self-worth, lack of 13
semi-structured interviews 100, 182
seminar programmes 196–7
significant others see critical friends
skilled helper model 112
small-scale research
  action research 198
  opportunities for ix
  questionnaire surveys 144, 147
social context, of research 81
social science research 128
software packages
  bibliographic 71
  data analysis 125
  data management 151
  statistical 167
sources, referencing 199–204
spreadsheets 151
stakeholders
  critical community 110, 118
  in professional development 13
standards, raising 14, 15, 22, 25, 28
statistical calculation 159–64
statistical software packages 167
Stenhouse, Lawrence 9
story telling 91, 92
story writing 43–6
strengths, SWOT analysis 42
structured interviews 100
structured reading 78–9

subcategories 133–4
subject knowledge 24
subject-specific journals 73
subjectivity 94
supervision
    critical pedagogy of 108–9
    of research x
support
    critical community 118
    critical friendship 110, 115
    for professional development 15
    for research 122–4
SWOT analysis 42
synopses 185
System for Classroom Observation of Teaching
        Strategies (SCOTS) 97
systematic inquiry 81, 169
systematic observation 95

tacit knowledge 10, 41, 44
talk, critical friendship 107
tally charts 149, 150, 164
tape recording, interviews 37, 129
Taylor & Francis Group 74
teacher biography interviews 100
teacher learning 18–20
Teacher Research Grant Scheme 75
Teacher Training Agency (TTA) 54, 58, 75
teachers
    development *see* professional development
    expectations of research 188–90
    identity *see* professional identity
    as researchers 9, 22, 24–6
teaching assistants 108
technical rationality 10
technical toolkits 87
telephone interviews 101
tensions
    in action research 26
    practitioner research 80
    professional development 15–16

theoretical frameworks 179–80
theoretical knowledge 115–16
theoretical sampling 136
theory
    developing 137–8
    referring to literature about 66
    scientific research 127
    tension between practice and 26
thought, recording 89–90
threats, SWOT analysis 42
time frames, diary/log/journal entries 90
time-sampling techniques 94
timelines, research topics 53
Times Educational Supplement 74, 75, 177
titles, research reports 174
toolkits, professional development 16
trial solutions 7, 8f
triangulation 85, 86f
truth 3, 4f, 6, 8, 116

United States
    professional development
        political battles 13–14, 15
        research on core features 18
Universities Council for the Education of
        Teachers (UCET) 75
unstructured interviews 101

validating groups 110
validation 45, 118, 135
validity 6, 7, 84, 118
value, of professional development activities 20–1
value judgements 97
verification 127, 128
videos 198

weakness, SWOT analysis 42
word documents 70–1
writing *see* reporting research

ZETOC 74